Be the Coolest
Dad on the Block

Be the Coolest
Dad on the Block

All of the Tricks, Games, Puzzles, and Jokes
You Need to Impress Your Kids
(and keep them entertained for years to come!)

Steve Caplin and Simon Rose

Broadway Books

New York

PRINTED IN THE UNITED STATES OF AMERICA

BROADWAY BOOKS and its logo, a letter B bisected on the diagonal, are trademarks of Broadway Books, a division of Random House, Inc.

Visit our Web site at www.broadwaybooks.com

Illustrations and book design by Steve Caplin

Library of Congress Cataloging-in-Publication Data

 Caplin, Steve.

 [Dad stuff]

 Be the coolest dad on the block : all of the tricks, games, puzzles, and jokes you need to impress your kids (and keep them entertained for years to come!) / Steve Caplin and Simon Rose.—1st Broadway Books trade pbk. ed.

  p. cm.

Originally published : Dad Stuff. London : Simon & Schuster, 2005.

Includes index.

 1. Fatherhood—Miscellanea. 2. Father and child—Miscellanea. 3. Amusements. 4. Creative activities and seat work. I. Rose, Simon. II. Title.

HQ756.C364 2006

306.874′2—dc22

2005054245

ISBN 0-7679-2249-2

10 9 8 7 6 5 4 3

Contents

This book is dedicated to our children: Joseph, Izzy, and Connie Rose; Freddy and Joe Caplin. And, of course, to their mothers, Jane and Carol, without whom they'd probably be filthy, unclothed, and starving.

Thanks to all those who offered their expertise, in particular: Martin Ball, Andy Best, Margaret Lawrence, Steph Lawrence, Shawn Sorrell, Catherine Christof, Robin Welch, Roger Jackson, all the Gallimores, Simon Trevor-Roberts, Fiona Tracey, Paul Caplin.

Finally, we'd like to thank Larry Page and Sergey Brin, without whom this book could never have been completed. They're the guys who created Google.

Introduction

WHEN STEVE'S FIRST CHILD was born, a friend gave him a mug inscribed *Anyone can be a FATHER, but it takes someone special to be a DAD.* This slushy, saccharine sentiment mystified him at the time. When you're up to your armpits in a sea of disposable nappies, strollers, and bottle sterilizers, and everything reeks of baby oil and vomit, it's hard enough just to keep going—let alone contemplate the forthcoming joys of fatherhood.

But as your children evolve from babies into kids, they cease seeing you merely as a supplier of powdered milk and poopless Pampers and acquire an interest in your bottomless fund of knowledge and experience. Almost from the moment they begin to talk, kids are asking questions. Questions to which you, no longer just their father but now their Dad, are expected to have instant, accurate, relevant, and entertaining answers.

And this is the problem. When our kids expect us to know everything, we really can't disappoint them. That can wait until their late teenage years, when they'll come to believe that everything we ever told them was either misguided nonsense or a cunningly constructed hodgepodge of mistruths calculated to repress their freedom of expression.

Until that fateful day, we have their full attention. We owe it to them, as well as to the whole of Dadkind, to preserve the myth that Dads are infallible, all-knowing, and as near omnipotent as a mortal can be.

We need to be able to fix their toys when they break, cheer them up when they're down, entertain them when they're bored, educate them when they're curious, and enlighten them when they're confused. We need to be able to juggle, to tie knots, to identify trees, and to do magic. We need to know why the sky is blue, why you can't dig a hole right through the earth, and what to do in a thunderstorm.

Above all, Dads need to be able to make childhood *fun*. Whether it's keeping them going on car journeys or organizing games to play in the park, a Dad should be an endless resource of ideas and inspiration.

None of us are perfect Dads, much as we'd like to be. And while Mums have an established tradition of comparing notes, medical histories, and intimate details of their relationships, Dads—by nature reserved and tight-lipped—have no such support group. We need a book to help us become the paragons to which we all aspire. Until we find it, this one will have to do.

Simon Rose and Steve Caplin, London, 2005

Anyone can be a FATHER but it takes someone special to be a DAD

1 Fun with everyday objects

PAPER BAGS, STRAWS, USED FILM CANISTERS, old hats, Ping-Pong balls, empty toilet paper rolls. A treasure trove of tools to be used by the resourceful Dad to amuse, entertain, and instruct even the most world-weary of Internet-age children.

When they're younger, kids will probably use this detritus to build fantasy castles and spaceships. As they become more inquisitive, it's Dad's turn to show them the true potential of these mundane castoffs.

These activities don't require complex construction, or whole afternoons spent knee-deep in modeling clay, polystyrene and sticky-back plastic. (There's plenty of that in a later chapter.) Some are spur-of-the-moment tricks and games. Others require just a little preparation—the chances, for instance, of happening upon a film canister and an indigestion tablet together are, at best, slight; it's wise to start saving these items for a rainy day whenever you come across them.

The ball you can't pick up

You walk toward a ball and reach down for it. But, every time, just as your hand is about to touch the ball, it flies off ahead of you as if it's trying to escape. It looks impressive, but is terribly simple.

As you walk toward the ball, pretend to try to grab it at the very moment your foot kicks it away. And if you don't have a ball, use a can.

Kick the ball as you reach to pick it up

No more than seven folds

It's not possible to fold a piece of paper in half more than seven times, no matter how big or thin it is. Naturally no child takes this piece of knowledge on trust. They are usually convinced that somehow they will be able to prove the rest of the world wrong with a sheet torn roughly from an exercise book and a firm press or two of a ruler.

As they will soon find, repeated doubling over of the paper means that, generally around the seventh fold, the paper becomes too thick to fold over any more.

Previous generations of children simply accepted this, much as they might accept that the Earth revolves around the sun. More recently, inquisitive minds have discovered that, using enormous sheets of thin paper, seven folds can be bettered.

Indeed, one precocious schoolkid, Britney Gallivan, studied the problem as a math project and found a way to fold paper 12 times. It involves some seriously complicated equations so we'll take her word for it.

The hole in your head hat trick

Don't worry, we're not going to suggest a spot of do-it-yourself cranial surgery. But you *can* convince smaller kids (and exceptionally gullible bigger ones) that you have a hole in the top of your head.

You need a hat with a hard brim. Something like a bowler, a top hat or a fireman's helmet would work well. So too should a bike helmet, though you may need to reverse it.

Stand against a wall with the brim of the hat touching it. Put your finger in your mouth and inflate your cheeks as if you're blowing hard. As you do so, push your head back slightly so that the brim of the hat is pressing gently against the wall. The front of the hat will rise.

After a moment, take out your finger, let the hat drop back and pretend to be really puffed with the exertion. Then do it again. You can even let your audience examine your head for signs of the hole.

You wouldn't smile either
if you had wooden teeth

Say "cheese," Mr. President

Want to make George Washington smile or frown at your command? Take any dollar bill and fold it backward vertically at the midpoint of his mouth. Fold it forward at each end of his mouth, making a small inverted V the full width of the note.

Without the V needing to be particularly pronounced, if you tilt the top of the banknote toward you, Washington will smirk. Tip it away and he is definitely not amused.

If you worry about exposing your children to temptation by handing them your hard-earned money, this trick can be done with pretty much any photo.

As strong as an egg

An egg? Strong? Indeed it is, amazingly so. Any architect would tell you how strong arches are and that domes are stronger still, which is why they're used in a variety of buildings from igloos to cathedrals.

And what is an egg, if not two domes joined together? Given the ease with which eggs break, you may be skeptical.

So try it. Place an uncooked egg upright into something soft and pliable, such as Silly Putty or a bunched-up tea towel. Put two piles of books of the same height

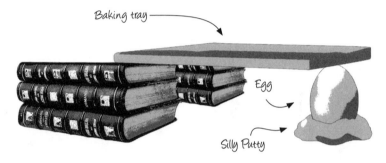

Baking tray

Egg

Silly Putty

nearby. Use them and the egg as a tripod on which to rest a light but solid sheet, such as a thin baking tray.

Gently place a thick book, then another, then another onto the tray. You and the kids will be surprised just how much weight the egg can bear before giving up the ghost. That's because the dome-like egg distributes the pressure evenly around its shell.

Another surprising example of an egg's strength is to wrap your fingers around one lengthways and squeeze it as hard as you can. If you're of a nervous disposition, you may prefer to do this outside or over the sink. Providing you remove any rings that could fracture the shell, the chances are that you won't be able to break the egg, no matter how hard you try. You can even get one or more children to squash your closed hand with all their might.

It worked for us, but bear in mind that we write and draw for a living, hardly occupations renowned for building up muscle strength. You won't find us of an evening tearing up telephone directories. If you've just returned from dragging a sled to the North Pole, you may succeed where we failed.

The Great Egg Trick

It was all so much easier in the olden days. Children were seen and not heard, called their father "Sir" and prefaced other adults' names with "Uncle" or "Auntie." How much trickier it is these days for Dads to keep their air of authority and superiority in this been-there, done-that, got-the-T-shirt-and-bundled-it-dirty-under-the-bed era.

If anything's going to restore the Dads of the world to mythic status in the eyes of their children, it's *The Great Egg Trick*. It isn't easy. In fact, it's fiendishly difficult. The chances are that you will fail. Totally, massively and messily.

But the failure will be so spectacular that your children are likely to talk about it for weeks to come. Make your attempt on *The Great Egg Trick* an annual event and your kids may bring their mates along to witness you getting egg on your face —and elsewhere.

Should you actually succeed in bringing it off, however, you will become a Dad among Dads, spoken of in hushed tones in parks and playgrounds. Other parents may approach you for your autograph, saying it's not for them but their little one. All you need is four eggs, four glasses, four tubes to hold the eggs, and a tray.

Practise with hard-boiled eggs by all means, but when you perform *The Great Egg Trick* in earnest they must be raw.

Place four tumblers or cups half full of water on a table, in a rectangular pattern. Place a tray with a lip onto the glasses or cups. If you're right-handed, have the tray protrude a little to the right (and vice versa).

You need something to hold the eggs. The outer part of matchboxes squashed into a more circular shape would do, or rolled-up index cards held together with rubber bands. Whatever you choose, it shouldn't be much shorter than the egg; the eggs should sit comfortably enough that they won't fall off if somebody breathes too heavily, but not so snugly that they'd still be there after a minor earthquake.

Examine these egg holders from all angles to ensure that they are positioned exactly above the tumblers and then carefully place the eggs onto them, as shown in the illustration.

You are now going to hit the tray out of the way, relying on inertia to keep the eggs in place long enough to plop down into the water. You can whack the tray with the flat of your hand or use a heavy book. Whatever your preferred method, you must give it enough of a knock that the tray flies clear. A quick, clean blow without a follow-through is what is needed, first ensuring that nobody is in the tray's flight path.

Get it right and you've nothing worse than four splashes of water to clear up. Get it wrong, and . . . well, there's always next year.

The broken egg on the head

We realize that most people must know this one, but there has to be a first time for every child. Place your hand, splayed, on the top of your child's head and tap your wrist with the fingers of the other hand. Inside the victim's head, it sounds exactly like an egg breaking.

Follow it by trailing your fingers lightly down the sides of their head, barely touching their hair. The whole effect is greatly enhanced if they see you holding an egg beforehand.

Other uses for eggs

We're told, on fairly reliable authority, that eggs can also be cooked and eaten. Seems like a waste of a good trick to us.

Balloon power

Many people know that if you rub an inflated balloon vigorously against your hair or wool clothing it will pick up static electricity and can then be stuck in place on a wall, ceiling, TV or even a face. The action of rubbing the balloon gives it extra negatively charged electrons. Other electrically neutral objects, such as a tin can, are more positively charged than the balloon, and because opposites attract, the two pull together.

You can get so much more fun from a statically charged balloon than simply sticking it on something. Hold it above your head, for instance, and your hair will

Bring a charged balloon near an empty can . . .

. . . and the can will roll toward it as if by magic!

stand up, with each positively charged, upstanding strand trying its hardest to get away from its neighbor. Hold it above a plate of salt, sugar or breakfast cereal and watch the stuff jump onto the balloon.

FASCINATING FACT

Static electricity helps explain lightning and has even powered a spaceship. Printers and photocopiers depend on it for fixing images. No doubt their inventors spent far too much time as kids sticking balloons to walls.

Even better, the charged balloon will attract water. Turn a tap on so there's a gentle trickle of water. Hold your balloon near it and the flow of water will bend toward the balloon, a neat way of enlivening bathtime.

Cooler still, the balloon will attract an empty soft-drink can strongly enough to get it to roll along a hard floor, pulling it in either direction. Get a couple of cans and you can have a race.

Piercing a balloon

Shove something sharp into an inflated balloon and you'd expect it to go bang. But if you put a bit of sticky tape on it first, you can insert a wooden barbecue skewer or pointy knitting needle without mishap. In fact, you can insert several, although the air will begin leaking out.

Stick another bit of tape on the other side of the balloon, and with care you can even pass the skewer or needle all the way through.

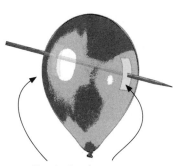

Tape both sides prevents skewers bursting the balloon

Standing on balloons without bursting them

Challenge your kids to see if they can stand on ordinary, inflated balloons without bursting them. Naturally, after a bout of noisy experimentation, they'll claim that it's impossible.

Not so, at least not if you use more than one balloon and spread your weight. Turn a tray upside down and use its ridge to secure the balloons beneath it.

Stand near something you can hold on to, such as a table or chair. While your children wince in expectation of four bangs, gingerly put first one foot onto the tray, then a little more weight and finally the other foot. You should be able to straighten up so that you are standing unaided on the tray.

Lip holds balloons in place

Going quackers

Flatten a plastic straw at one end. Cut a little away at both sides of the flattened end so that the straw has a V-shaped point. Put the straw a little way into your mouth,

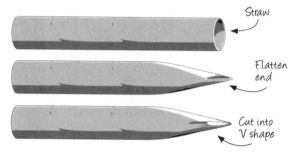

blow hard and, after a little experimentation, you should be rewarded with a satisfying duck sound.

Push another straw into the other end and, although harder to blow, you should be able to produce a much lower note, more moose than mallard.

When service in a fast food joint isn't as speedy as you'd like, getting your whole party to quack together (using the straws thoughtfully provided for this purpose) should do wonders for speeding up your order.

The jumping paper clips

Fold a dollar bill in three so that, edge on, it looks like a Z. Place one paper clip half an inch or so in from the left end, fastening it to the middle section and front; fasten another half an inch in from the right, fixed to the back and middle sections. (If you place the paper clips on the wrong sections, it won't work.) You should push both paper clips right down —they're only left sticking up in the illustration so you can see where they are better.

Grasp the two side ends of the note and pull. The paper clips will spring off. No surprise there. But when you retrieve them, you'll discover that they are magically linked together.

In the bag

Paper bags are great for catching all manner of invisible things. Hang on to any you get while out shopping. They aren't as common as they once were, but you still get them occasionally.

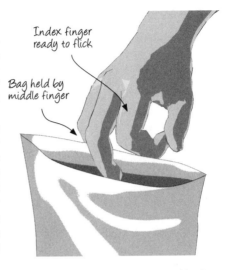

Index finger ready to flick

Bag held by middle finger

Hold the bag with your middle finger inside it and your index finger held back by your thumb. Throw the whateveritis up in the air, following its trajectory with your eyes. As it drops into the bag, flick it with your index finger. Both the noise and the sudden movement will make it seem as if something really has fallen into the bag.

Paper bags are also brilliant for blowing up and bursting. Childish? Not a bit of it. It's an excellent demonstration of how thunder occurs.

I see no ships

The hole in the hand

Hold an empty toilet paper tube to one eye and look straight ahead at something in the distance.

Bring your free hand up toward your other eye. As it comes alongside the tube, it should look as if there's a round hole in your hand, through which you can see whatever you were looking at.

If you don't have an empty toilet paper tube, then either empty one (see page 96 for a great reason to do this), or else use a sheet of paper rolled up and kept circular with the hand.

Forever blowing bubbles

Children needn't despair if they lose the plastic bubble wand that came with their bubbles, or have run out of bubble solution. Both are easy to replace. You can make your own liquid from one part dishwashing liquid to about twelve parts of water. You'll get even better bubbles if you mix a little sugar in, though the water will need to be warm to dissolve it.

Putting the mixture into a clean bowl (dirt is bad for bubbles) makes everything so much easier. You can press umpteen handy objects into service as bubble-makers; bent wire (experiment with shapes), straws (use paper clips to fasten them together into shapes), a fly swatter, plastic strawberry baskets, the plastic bit holding your six-pack of beer together.

You can even use your hands. Overlap your thumbs with your index fingers touching to make a triangle. It's dryness rather than sharpness that pops bubbles, so make sure you soak your hands in the solution. This way you can also hold bubbles *on* your hands without them bursting.

If you're after giant bubbles then make a bubble loop. Slip a couple of straws onto a length of string and tie it into a loop, concealing the knot in one of the straws. Holding the straws, make a rectangular shape, dip it into your solution and gently waft it through the air. A length of fabric tape about six feet long, weighed down with something like a nut or a washer, is another good way of making a bubble loop—though it'll need two of you to open the loop.

If you've a kiddie pool and a hula hoop, put the hoop over something in the middle a child can stand on. When they're in position, bring up the hoop and the child will be in the middle of a giant bubble!

Nut to weigh down fabric

2 Batteries not required

"DAD, I'M BORED." Once, those words would have struck terror into your heart. No more. After all, you now have drawers bursting with Ping-Pong balls, balloons, paper clips, straws, sticky tape, old newspapers, rubber bands, and more. You are as prepared as a forward-thinking Dad can be.

But what if you aren't at home when they're getting restless? Don't panic. Resourceful as you are, you still retain the ability to divert, instruct and amuse with nothing more than the body Nature gave you. It may not be the trim, slick model of perfection it once was, but as an entertainer of children it has no equal.

Here is a range of games and pastimes requiring no preparation or props whatsoever, yet which will still amaze and delight even the most jaded of childish imaginations. Some are educational, some amusing, many are downright daft. Some were favorites of our playground days, ready to be dusted off and rereleased to an entirely new generation. All should be part of your ever-expanding arsenal of activities to counter boredom.

Going up

Press down hard (but not *too* hard) on someone's head for 10 seconds. Ask them to shut their eyes while you put your hands under their arms and make as if you're lifting them into the air. Without actually trying to bear their weight, they will get the impression that they have been lifted clear of the ground.

Similarly, pin their arms by their sides while they try hard to push outward. After 10 seconds, tell them to stop. When you let go, their arms will involuntarily float up into the air.

The incredible shrinking arm (1)

Who can resist the seemingly impossible challenge of lengthening their own limbs? Unlike expensive plastic surgery, this method's 'armless—and the effect is, mercifully, temporary.

Hold your arms out horizontally in front of you, palms touching. As our arms tend to be the same length, your two middle fingers should be the same distance away from you. With one hand, vigorously rub the upper part of the arm still outstretched for four or five seconds. Now hold the two arms out together.

Suddenly the one you've rubbed is longer than the other. Or is it that the other one is now shorter?

You can expect your rubbed arm to be about an inch longer!

The incredible shrinking arm (2)

Here's an interesting variation on the same trick. Stand facing a wall with both arms stretched out, palms flat against the wall.

Now make a sweeping circular motion with one arm, swinging it backward over your head and back to its starting position. This hand will no longer reach the wall!

Mind the gap!

Blinkety blink

That hallowed time-waster, seeing who can hold off blinking the longest, has actually now become a sport. There are staring face-off competitions with proper rules and giant video screens that project the contestants' faces to the audience.

Set up your own domestic championship. Each competing pair rests their elbows on the table and stares into each other's eyes. At the bell (or tambourine, squeaky mouse or whatever's at hand), they must refrain from touching, talking, laughing, yawning, moving suddenly or even smiling. The first to blink is the loser.

Astoundingly, the record for not blinking is currently over 22 minutes. So get your kids practicing now. It surely can't be long before it's an Olympic sport, along with *Thumb Wars* and *Rock, Paper, Scissors*.

The invisible bonds

Get your victim to put their hands together. Then tell them that you are tying their hands together, and mime winding string around their hands, around and around and around. As you do it, tell them that their hands are being forced ever more tightly together.

Round and round you go, until you finally tie off the string. Then say you're going to set them free. Mime cutting the string with scissors. If it has worked, they should find it oddly difficult to pull their hands apart.

A related piece of weirdness is to get someone to hold out their arms with their hands six inches or so apart. With your index finger extended, circle their outstretched hands with one of yours, getting faster and faster. They will find it very difficult not to bring their hands ever closer together.

The comedy trip

"Beware of the invisible rope," you warn, either indoors or out. The kids search for it, but naturally can't find it. Yet, whenever you pass the spot, it trips you up.

It's pretty easy to do. Simply walk normally. As you get to the chosen spot, knock the foot that's coming forward into the heel of the other foot. You will trip convincingly, but with little danger of falling flat on your face. It's pretty hard to spot how it's done, so you can repeat it for ages before, if you're so inclined, letting them in on the secret.

Rock, Paper, Scissors . . . gun

Bang! is a shooting variation on *Rock, Paper, Scissors* that has an element of subtlety and tension that's absent from the original game: it can also be played by more than two players.

From two to five players sit in a circle. Tapping their hands on their knees, they all count 1–2–3 then raise their hands in one of three gun positions, aiming at one of the other players. Both hands pointing forward means Shoot; crossed across the chest means Shield; raised to the shoulders means Reload.

If you shoot someone who's reloading or shooting someone else, you win a point. If you shoot someone who's shielding, there's no score; if you shoot someone who's shooting you, both players' scores are reduced to zero.

You must reload each time before you can shoot, but if you reload twice you will get two consecutive shots. The game gets quicker as the players get accustomed to it, and is won by the first player to get five points.

If you're sitting around a table, *Bang!* can be played by rapping closed knuckles on the table during the count.

Tap three times on your knees

Shield

Shoot

Reload

Sofa my next trick . . .

Who said mimes aren't funny? The sofa

Forbid the kids from going into the secret cellar, located behind the sofa or couch, or whatever you call that long piece of furniture you doze on after a good lunch. When you go behind it into the cellar, simply walk behind it, getting lower in jumpy stages as if you're descending steps. Once you've completely disappeared from sight, turn round and come back up again.

Why this should be such a source of wonderment to young minds remains a mystery, but it's there for Dads to take advantage of. You can even install an escalator to make your journey that much smoother. Try canoeing along a hidden river, too, jerking forward as you dig your paddle in.

Who said mimes aren't funny? The elevator

If you encounter a frosted glass door with a solid bottom half then, with your audience on the other side, press the imaginary down button. By bending your knees you can appear to be slowly "descending" to another floor.

You can mime the elevator getting stuck between floors and jiggling you up and down as the machine struggles to free itself. As the *pièce de résistance*, press the button again and, with a bemused expression, find yourself being bizarrely carried off to the side and out of sight.

Who said mimes aren't funny? The kiss

Rodin's *The Kiss* may be a masterpiece of French sculpture, but it doesn't get many laughs. Turn your back to an audience and you can pretty convincingly make it look as if somebody is kissing you.

Simply wrap your arms around your body with your fingertips reaching onto your back and, making appropriate noises if desired, move your hands up and down. Perhaps this is best done in reasonable proximity to your other half, unless you fancy explaining when you get home why the kids saw you kissing somebody in the park.

Who said mimes aren't funny? The strangler

Not all our ideas are cribbed from old TV comedians (see page 64), but it was certainly Eric Morecambe of the 1970s British show *Morecambe and Wise* who first

It's curtains for me

demonstrated the potential of the phantom strangler to us.

Baring your arm to the halfway mark, grab your own throat, ensuring that your elbow is hidden behind a wall or curtain from your audience's point of view. Make it look as though you're struggling against the hand's attempts to pull you away, using the other hand to give the impression you're trying to free yourself. Simple, but very effective.

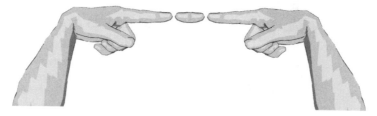

Spectral sausages

With your hands some way apart and roughly nine inches from your eyes, point your index fingers at each other. As you look at something in the distance, gradually bring your fingers toward each other. When they're just a few inches apart, a ghostly "sausage" should appear in midair in between your two fingers.

Banging your head on a wall

There are surely times when your offspring make you feel like indulging in a gentle session of headbanging, not to soothing heavy metal music, but against a nearby wall.

You can get all the benefits of this time-honored method of relieving frustration without any of the usual danger of bruising, lumps or stitches.

As your head comes close, but not quite into contact with the wall, kick your foot into the base to make the corresponding knocking sound. This works particularly well with the resonant bases of kitchen units. If you chose to economize when you had them installed, a gentle tap might prove to be more sensible than a full-blooded goal kick.

Weird handshakes

Shake your child's hand. At the last minute, tuck your middle finger in so it rests against your palm. "Don't mind the wart," you say as they squirm.

Other handshake jokes involve shaking in the manner of different professions: say "I'm a dairy farmer" as you repeatedly squeeze their fingers; "I'm a train driver" as you pump your arm back and forth like a piston; "I'm from the electricity company" as you vibrate your middle finger; "I'm from the Left Handed Society" as you extend your left hand toward their right; "I'm a submarine captain" as you make to shake their hand, then duck yours beneath at the last moment.

Burping the alphabet

Instead of chanting at the kids, for the umpteenth time, "Don't do that," try to out-gross them from time to time. Hard to do, it's true, but you should at least be able to sink to somewhere approaching their level by challenging them to a "burp the alphabet" contest.

If you don't already know how to burp intentionally, it's a bit tricky to learn, though we're sure you can easily find children willing to teach you. There's a sort of tiny swallow involved inside your throat. Connie, our resident young professor of burping, advises that you need to "burp in, then burp out."

Once you can do it, you have to sound out a letter as you burp it. Like ventriloquism, certain letters are easier and others harder. The soft ones like "C," "J" and "S" are tricky, the vowels a breeze.

It's possible that other, less enlightened souls may find a group of kids burping the alphabet, even with a supposed grown-up in attendance, a bit offensive. In that case, you mustn't forget your manners. Everyone should remember to say "pardon" after each burp.

Thumb wars

This cut-down version of arm wrestling is a great time-occupier if there aren't any handy distractions. Bend your four fingers inward and interlock your hand with that of your opponent. Both move your thumbs in alternate, opposite directions as you chant, "1–2–3–4, I declare a thumb war."

Then, hands still locked together, each must try to press down their opponent's thumb with their own and hold it down.

Thumb you win, thumb you don't . . .

Levitation for beginners

Get this right and, in an amazing feat, four children will lift an adult into the air using only their index fingers. The adult should sit upright on a hard chair, arms folded, while four children (aged eight years up seems to work fine) stand next to it, two ready to lift under the arms and two under the knees.

Under both arms...

...and under the knees

The four should first attempt to lift the adult by clasping their hands and putting their index fingers together. Not surprisingly, they probably won't be able to budge the person at all.

The children should then stretch their right hands in turn above the victim's head followed by their respective left hands. They need to keep their hands there for a short while, counting to 10, or chanting some mumbo-jumbo over and over such as "2, 4, 6, 8, Who are we to levitate?" or whatever takes their fancy.

After 10–15 seconds, they drop their hands and immediately lift the person with their joined index fingers. Miraculously, they should be able to raise the person several inches from the chair. (Just what we need, kids finding yet another way of getting a rise out of an adult.)

This didn't work *every* time we tried it. Some practitioners claim it works better if the children actually put their hands on the victim's head and press down gently. Others say it's best if the chanting is of a more mystical bent. We find the whole thing somewhat perplexing. It's worth persevering, though, because when it does work, it really is utterly extraordinary.

Bet you can't do this

Everyone knows that it's tricky to rub your stomach and pat your head at the same time. But it's not *that* tricky. Certainly not as tricky as this.

With your arms extended, point your index fingers at each other. With one arm, draw a circle in the air, returning to the same point. Now do it with both arms, but in opposite directions. Your fingers ought to pass each other at the bottom and the top of the circle.

When you've mastered that, try circling your arms at different speeds, in opposite directions, then going the same way. Lastly, and this is the one we still can't quite get right, try moving one hand inside the orbit of the other, again trying both directions.

If you think this is childish, we'd like to point out that it was apparently thought up by Nobel Prize–winning theoretical physicist and inveterate practical joker Richard Feynman. So there! Incidentally, when Feynman's mum once heard him referred to as the "smartest man in the world," her response was, "If that's the world's smartest man, God help us!"

Once your kids master this, you can always bet them that they can't lick their elbow. This is pretty well impossible for most people, though naturally nobody takes this on trust until they've made themselves look mildly ridiculous by trying it out. It is, however, apparently an urban myth that nobody can do it. The *Guinness Book of Records* receives several claims a day from people who can, indeed, lick their own elbows.

Doing the Quofit

We've christened this the *Quofit* because we've no idea what this method of traveling sideways is really called. It's fun, though, and a good test of coordination.

Start with your heels together and your toes pointing outward. To travel to the right, pivot your right foot on your toe and your left foot on the heel until the toes

come together. Put your feet down and, in a continuous motion, pivot on your right heel and left toe until the heels are together again. Now keep going—if you can. Then try traveling backward.

Once you've all mastered it, put on some music and you're doing the Quofit.

And now the news and weather

This is one of our all-time favorites. It's daft in the extreme but invariably has us all in stitches. Best carried out with an audience, one person elects to be

the newscaster while another gets behind them and puts their arms through, ready to do all the actions. It doesn't seem to matter whether the puppeteer can be seen or not.

The newsreader (Dad may want to get the ball rolling) should talk about things that can easily be illustrated visually. As we hear about people being stabbed or strangled, for instance, the hands are showing us just that. When the police are puzzled, the hands can rub the chin or scratch the head. Frankly, when we're in a giggly mood, even an itchy leg being scratched will set us off.

If more children want to be involved, you can simulate a TV interview, with one of them asking questions and another doing the actions. Or you can swap and have a try at it yourself. You can even adapt it for telling bedtime stories with the help of an older sibling.

The dematerializing knees

From a spectator's point of view, it looks as though your knees are passing through each other and coming out the other side. No *Star Trek* wizardry is involved, however, just a plain simple parlor trick of old.

You'll need a bit of slow-motion practice before you trundle it out. Sitting down, plant your feet firmly on the ground close together. Put your hands on your knees and bring your knees together. Stretch your thumbs and index fingers across and place them on the other knee, one hand in front of the other, and lift off the other fingers. As you pull your knees apart, your hands should now continue their journey on their new knees.

The knees should continue out then back again. As they come together this time, transfer your outer fingers across to the other knee and continue as the hands return to their original position.

As you get up to speed and find that you can do it without thinking, the continuous motion of the hands as they cross and uncross makes it appear that your legs have crossed over. Before long, you should be able to do this standing up as well.

The broken nose trick

This is another great way to gross out your kids. Claim that you can dislocate or break your nose whenever you want. With your thumbs in your mouth, place your hands either side of your nose. Quickly bend them (and your nose) to one side, at the same time flicking your thumbnails against your front teeth to make a clicking sound. Then reset it, moving it back to its original position, again flicking your teeth.

Exhaustive research with a tape recorder and headphones (we may be sad, but at least we are *thorough*) reveals that the aperture of the mouth is important, as the interior acts as an amplifier. Don't leave it wide open: instead, hold it in a relaxed position, with just a slight gap between your lower lip and your thumbnails.

Cheeky music

Slapping your cheeks with open palms (preferably your own) makes an elementary sort of music. Adjust the opening and shape of your mouth and cheeks to change the pitch. After a somewhat bruising testing session, it turns out that Simon's mouth has a range of an octave, which makes it perfect, for instance, for accompanying nursery rhymes. *Baa Baa Black Sheep* works particularly well: we recommend you don't move on to grand opera without medical insurance.

Making a noise like a pigeon

In the list of animals it would be cool to impersonate, the pigeon must come pretty well near the bottom. Unfortunately, we have no idea how to roar convincingly like a lion, neigh like a horse or warble like a nightingale. So, dull and commonplace though it may be, you'll have to settle for re-creating the soft mellifluous cooing of the pigeon.

Place the palms of your hands together at 90°, right over left. Curl your fingers around the opposite hand. Open up a gap between your hands but, at the same time, try to avoid any holes in what will be the sounding box.

Keeping them parallel, place the end of your thumbs on your right index finger. Bend the knuckles of your thumbs out a little, placing your mouth either side of them. Now blow softly: oo–*oo*–oo, oo–oo is the proper sequence.

Cooing like a pigeon, it turns out, is not quite like riding a bike. Even if you were a demon pigeon cooer in your youth, it can take a while in adulthood to

get a sound at all, and even then it may sound like the sort of bird that might have asthma from roosting too near a chemicals factory.

Persevere, though, and with luck your skills will improve. Above all, you must ensure that you're blowing softly. If you really find it difficult, console yourself with the knowledge that while Simon can conjure up a perfect pigeon at the drop of a feather, despite his expert tutelage Steve remains to this day entirely unable to produce a single warble.

The unsupported circle

If you have eight or more people with nothing to do, get them to stand up and form themselves into a tight circle, each person facing the back of the next person, only a few inches separating them.

Slowly, everyone should lower themselves until they are sitting on the knees of the person behind. It may take one or two tries but you should be able to create a circle with everyone sitting on somebody else's knees and the entire ring rock solid, even though nothing is actually holding it up.

A capital trick

Bet your kids that you are so brainy that you know every capital in the world. Get them to ask you the capital of any country, anywhere on Earth, or even any state capital.

They might try to trip you up with a difficult one and demand to know something like the capital of Kyrgyzstan. "That's easy," you say. "It's 'K.'" "The capital of Mississippi?" "M."

There'll be groans and they'll refuse to shell out on the bet. But you can bet they'll be trying it on their friends in school the next day.

The phantom hand

Hold your hand up against your child's, palms flat, thumbs together. Get them to stroke the middle finger and thumb of their *other* hand up and down a pair of fingers—one of yours and one of theirs.

The effect is rather spooky: to the child doing the stroking, they can feel one of the hands from the "inside," but not the other one. They know it's there, but it's as if they can't fully sense it. It works particularly well if they also close their eyes.

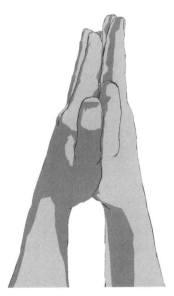

Jiving fingers

Our parents lived in a wacky age when you couldn't carry music around with you piped directly into your ears. In early pop concerts where they sat well-behaved, or in crowded diners or cafés where dancing to the jukebox was frowned upon, they would hand-jive instead.

There are still places where a hand-jive is more appropriate than strutting your stuff in full view of others. From your children's point of view, that's no doubt *everywhere* ("No, Dad! Not where people can *see*."). Ideally suited to rock'n'roll or swing, you need to select four different hand movements from those available. Most are done leading first with the right hand, then the left and repeating both before changing to another "step." The four movements are cycled in the same order over and over again. Hand-jiving with a couple of kids is great fun and is relatively unlikely to involve any embarrassing age-related dancing injury on the Dad's part.

Among the movements to pick from are:

- Holding one elbow with the other palm while you draw a circle in the air with your index finger.
- Passing the right hand over the left in a scissor-like motion twice.
- Holding your forearms parallel to each other, then spinning them around each other one way, then the other.
- Hitting your fists together twice, beginning right fist on top.
- Hitting your palms on your legs twice, then clapping twice.
- A hitchhiking motion, satrting with thumbs going outward.

Get the kids to come up with some more. Give them names, then they can "call" the dance as you go along.

3 The rubber band: a Dad's best friend

SOME WILL TELL YOU that a man's best friend is his dog. But dogs need feeding, walking, and, occasionally, neutering. The rubber band requires no such time-consuming attention, but will always help you out. About the only thing it won't do is rescue you from a snowdrift with a barrel of brandy round its neck.

Invented in 1845 by London coachmaker Stephen Perry, the rubber band is useful for all manner of temporary repairs, will hold things together while glue dries, is an essential component of catapults, a power source for small model planes and boats, a primitive musical instrument, a stress reliever and can even, apparently, be used for treating hemorrhoids (although this isn't recommended as a DIY procedure).

It used to be that you could never lay your hands on a rubber band when you needed one. But that was in the days before the Postal Service decided to distribute them, free, to every household in the land, bound around bundles of junk mail. If you can't find one, just wander down your street. Chances are, the postman will conveniently have left some lying on the pavement for you.

Chopsticks for butterfingers

Few things are more frustrating to the hungry child than a plate of steaming food and a pair of chopsticks they can't use. Out comes your trusty rubber band, which you use to fasten the chopsticks together near the top.

Roll up the wrapper the chopsticks came in and shove it between the chopsticks, just below the top rubber band. Now the chopsticks will be far easier to use, springing apart between food grabs rather like tweezers. If you're not too nifty with chopsticks yourself, you can also try it, claiming you're doing it so as not to show up your kids.

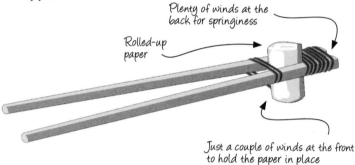

Plenty of winds at the back for springiness

Rolled-up paper

Just a couple of winds at the front to hold the paper in place

The best way to fire a rubber band

Hang a rubber band off the tip of your little finger. Shape your hand as if you're simulating a gun, with the thumb and index finger extended and the other fingers curled. With your other hand, stretch the rubber band around the base of your

thumb and over the center of your index finger. To fire the band, simply move your little finger.

As the band slips from your little finger, it will whip around your thumb and rocket off your index finger. Rubber bands fired this way have been clocked at 11 miles an hour and distances of over 20 feet should pose no problem.

The anti-gravity escalator

Snap or cut a rubber band so you have one long piece. You need something to slip over it. A wedding ring will do, but a paper clip is equally fine.

Thread this "passenger" onto the band, keeping it near your right hand. Holding the backs of your hands toward your audience, hide the better part of the band in the palm of your left hand and stretch the rest of the rubber band between the thumb and forefinger of each hand.

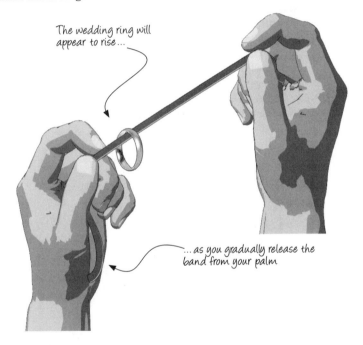

The wedding ring will appear to rise...

...as you gradually release the band from your palm

Raise your right hand until the passenger slides down toward your left hand, showing the effect of gravity. Keep the right hand raised. As you use your powerful, telekinetic eyes to defeat gravity—or whatever voodoo you invoke—let the hidden part of the rubber band gently slip through your left thumb and forefinger. Hey presto! The passenger will appear to be climbing up the rubber band.

The amazing jumping rubber band

With just a little practice, you can make a rubber band jump "magically" from your first two fingers to your outside two fingers in the blink of an eye.

Put a rubber band over your index finger and middle finger, positioning it at their base. With the back of your hand to the audience, pull the band to the outside of your hand on the pretext of showing that it's only a standard rubber band. As you're doing it, bend all four fingers down, and put the ends through the band.

Straighten your fingers out quickly and immediately clench them again: the rubber band will appear to jump in an instant to your ring finger and pinky. Stretch the band back the other way, curl your fingers through once more, straighten them, and it has jumped back again.

This trick can be made to look even more impressive. After slipping the rubber band over the two fingers, twist another rubber band around the tops of all four fingers. Pulling the fingers together, this will appear to "imprison" the first rubber band and make the jump seem that much more miraculous.

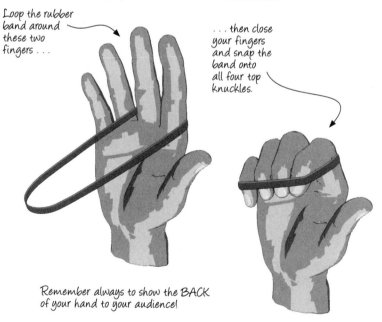

Loop the rubber band around these two fingers . . .

. . . then close your fingers and snap the band onto all four top knuckles.

Remember always to show the BACK of your hand to your audience!

The rubber band booby trap

Here's a great way to surprise any unsuspecting passerby. Take two pieces of paper rolled into cylinders (short pencils work just as well) and loop a thick rubber band round their centers. Twist one at least 20 times, propeller-fashion, until the rubber band is good and tight.

Place the entire assembly beneath a large or heavy object—a book, shirt, box of chocolates, for example—so that it's fully concealed. When someone lifts the object off, the rubber band assembly will spring into life with a clattering sound, as if a small but noisy animal had been released.

Making a rubber band ball

A handy way of keeping track of all your rubber bands is to combine them into a rubber band ball. Knot a rubber band until it is as compact as possible. Put another band around it, twisting it as needed to keep it in place. Keep doing this with successive bands until you no longer need to twist them.

Feed me!
Feed me!

You can cheat at the start by using a crumpled piece of paper or tinfoil as the core. If you fancy a particularly bouncy rubber band ball, put a superball at the center. Assuming you remember what a superball is, of course.

Although the presence of a rubber band ball in the home means you can always find a rubber band, children (or Dads) with an obsessive or compulsive nature should be discouraged from starting one. There is stiff competition for the title of the world's largest rubber band ball. The current record holder comprises more than half a million bands, has been over four years in the making, is five feet high and weighs over a ton!

FASCINATING FACT

After five years of making his rubber band ball, the previous record holder, Welshman Tony Evans, became curious to see how high it would bounce. The giant ball was dropped from a cargo plane a mile up over the Mojave Desert. Sadly, it did not bounce at all. Instead, once the 20-foot cloud of dust cleared, it revealed a four-foot-wide rubbery crater which survives to this day.

Building a rubber band tank

Before the more militaristically minded kids get too excited at the prospect of making a tank, it should be stressed that this one is more akin to an unsophisticated prototype of a World War I tank than, say, a modern M1A2 Abrams with turbine engine and Chobham armor.

You need a spool of thread, a couple of used matches, a candle stub about half an inch long and, naturally, the ubiquitous rubber band.

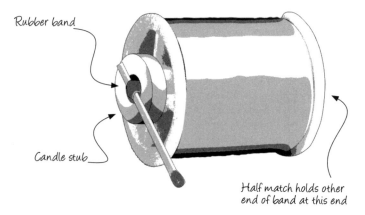

Rubber band

Candle stub

Half match holds other end of band at this end

Use a skewer or dawl to carefully make a hole in the candle stub, and push one end of the rubber band through the hole just far enough to push a match through. Pass the other end of the rubber band through the spool. Fix that end of the band in place with a match that's been snapped in half.

The long match is what "drives" the tank. Position it so that only a tiny part of the match is on one side of the rubber band. Then, using the long end of the match, wind up the rubber band. When it's as tight as it can go without the risk of snapping, place the tank on a smooth surface with the match touching the ground. The tank will begin trundling along as the rubber band begins to unwind itself.

FASCINATING FACT

One of the rubber-band powered flying models created by Frenchman Alphonse Penaud in the 1870s was given as a present by Bishop Milton Wright to his two young sons, Orville and Wilbur. They later claimed it was this toy flying helicopter that sparked their interest in powered flight.

4 Here's one I made earlier

KIDS LOVE MAKING THINGS. From model airplanes to Lego houses, from potato heads to matchstick models, few things generate such a sense of satisfaction as presenting their parents with something they've crafted themselves.

Sometimes they need Dad's help to get started. It's unlikely most kids would realize how to make animated movies on their own, for instance. But, once they're shown how it's done, they can go on to create further masterpieces unaided.

Best of all, though, is the stuff they can make from the most unlikely of raw materials: who would have thought you could make a kite from a garbage bag? Or a battleground for toy soldiers from a sheet of Styrofoam? Or a rocket from an empty film canister and an Alka-Seltzer tablet?

This section also has some stuff where Dads will have to do the hard work—such as the homemade garden swing and longbow —though it will be the kids that get the benefit.

Dioramas for model soldiers

Most boys have at least a hundred model soldiers. (Girls don't tend to play with soldiers until they're very much older.) They'll range from cheap, badly molded sets bought for $1 for 20 from the local convenience store, to lovingly hand-painted (and hugely expensive) Warhammer models.

But what use are all these soldiers without somewhere to display and play with them? Building a large diorama is fun for both Dad and kids, and is an activity that can be spread over several evenings and weekends. Best of all, the whole thing can be made for less than the cost of a typical Warhammer set.

Begin with a Styrofoam sheet for the base. You can buy sheets 4 feet square from craft stores: get them to cut it in half for you, so you have two pieces measuring 4 feet by 2 feet. One will serve as the base; the other is the ground level on top of this, in which you can carve out rivers, potholes, trenches, and bomb craters.

Styrofoam is a great modeling material to work with. It can easily be cut with a knife for a hard edge, which is great for making trenches; but scratch away the top layer with your fingers and something marvelous happens. That smooth, flat surface turns into a stony, lumpy piece of waste ground. Cut a chunk of river out, then crumble the edges to make the banks; turn pieces of crumbled-away surface upside down to make rocky outcrops of rough boulders that now have a perfectly smooth underside for fixing onto the ground. Shape pieces to make bridges, and

Crumble away
potholes with
your fingers

Cut a river from the top sheet

houses, and sections of broken wall. You can glue the pieces down with white glue or wallpaper paste, or just pin them in place with small nails. If you're feeling brave, drip plastic model cement onto the model to melt away potholes.

To make the riverbed, lay a piece of tinfoil between the two main sheets of polystyrene before you glue them together. This will give a good reflective appearance. Then paint it blue or gray with felt pens, ink or translucent paints or stains: a couple of coats of glue on top will build up a good thick shine. Drip glue into bomb craters to flood them. Use household objects for their texture: corrugated cardboard, with the top layer peeled away, makes a great roofing material; ice-cream sticks can be turned into fences; coils of wire make convincing barbed wire.

The model should first be painted dark gray or black overall, using a matte water-based household paint. This creates a good base color, and protects the polystyrene from further damage. Then use those little tester pots of paint (the ones with a built-in brush are best) to dab color onto the walls, masonry, and grass. Short, stabbing actions of two different greens make the best grass, and the technique works well for house walls as well.

The best moment of all is when your son's friends come to visit. "*I made that,*" he'll announce proudly, "*with my Dad.*"

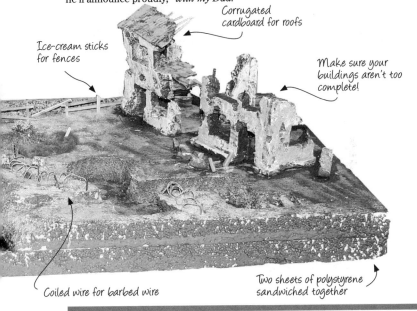

Corrugated cardboard for roofs

Ice-cream sticks for fences

Make sure your buildings aren't too complete!

Coiled wire for barbed wire

Two sheets of polystyrene sandwiched together

How to take 3-D photographs with any camera

With children reared on a diet of special effects–driven Hollywood blockbusters, it's getting ever harder to impress them with mere photographs.

Three-D photography could do the trick. Whether taking pictures with real film* or a digital camera, the technique is the same. Find a scene which has some foreground elements as well as a significant distant feature. Take one shot, preferably using the camera in the portrait position—vertical rather than horizontal.

Try it for yourself. You may find it easier to see if you place a piece of card here

Take a step to one side and take another shot of the same view, keeping the background feature in roughly the same place in the viewfinder.

To view the images in 3D, place the photos side by side with a piece of card between them. The viewer should bring his face toward the photographs so that his nose is in line with and almost touching the card.

The technique also works if you display the images side by side on a computer screen, holding a bit of card in place. It may be sensible to switch the screen to a higher resolution, making the images smaller so that they melt together more easily. If you don't have any card, the images can also be viewed by deliberately going wall-eyed (the opposite of cross-eyed), but this can take a bit of practice.

Children amazed by this should know that it really is nothing new. It's simply a variation of the Victorian stereoscopes popular 150 years ago.

Keep the film canisters—see page 44.

Möbius and his performing strips

Cut a strip of paper along the long side—an inch or so wide—and twist it once before sticking it together to form a loop. The longer the strip is, the easier the loop will be to play with.

Ask a child to draw a red line down the middle of one side, and a blue line down the other. They'll soon realize it can't be done. There is only one side. Mark a spot on the edge with a pencil or a paper clip and they'll discover it also has only one edge.

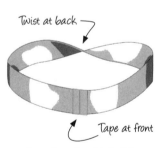

Twist at back

Tape at front

Cut the strip down the middle all the way around, asking what they think will happen. They'll suspect it will become two loops. In fact, you end up with just one loop, half the width and double the length of the first (and with four twists in it).

Create another loop, a little wider than before and cut along it a third of the way in. After a while you'll find you're cutting two-thirds of the way across to form one long cut. You end up with one long strip and one shorter one.

This wackiness was discovered in 1858 by two German mathematicians independently, August Ferdinand Möbius and Johann Benedict Listing. Listing got there first, by two months, but the immortality went to Möbius, presumably because everyone thought his name was far cooler.

How to make animated movies

Although we talk of "movies," what we're really watching is a rapid succession of still images (24 a second on film, 30 on TV and video). Thanks to an effect known as persistence of vision, our brain is fooled into thinking it looks real.

It isn't difficult to make basic animated movies with your kids, even if you only have a standard video camera. It doesn't need to be digital, though that does make editing easier. It's handy if you can set it to record only when the button is quickly depressed—you want to film just a couple of frames at a time. The principle behind any stop-motion animated movie is the same. Run the camera very briefly, move whatever you're shooting slightly, run the camera momentarily again, move your subject a little and so on, over and over again.

A good starting point is to video building blocks. Film nothing first, then put a block in the frame, film it quickly, put another in shot, film again, then bring in another block, shoot it and just keep going until you've completed a wall, tower or life-size model of the Empire State Building. Make sure the base and camera stay absolutely still!

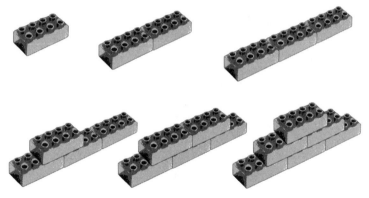

When it's seen building itself, even the simplest model seems magical

Screen what you've filmed and the effect is extraordinary, particularly with young children. You're a sorcerer. You've taken something incredibly familiar to them, something they play with every day, and brought it magically to life. Blocks appear out of thin air, one after another, and a pyramid or whatever is constructed with no visible human intervention.

The next stage is up to you. Start with something already built and have it vanish, brick by brick. Make something from construction bricks and gradually transform it into something else. Paint a diorama for a background and move wheeled models in front of it. Film pliable figures, made from modeling clay, moving them incrementally for each shot. Scenarios can be written, storyboards planned and drawn, costumes and sets made, music added. It may all seem very basic by the standards of Pixar movies, but this is how Wallace and Gromit were born.

The films you make together may get more sophisticated, but it's unlikely you'll ever achieve the thrill the children get when their building blocks first come to life on the TV screen.

Making a bow and arrow

Building a bow should be simple: you just take a stick and bend it, right? Wrong. Unless you live by a forest that grows planed, seasoned yew trees, bending sticks won't give you anything like the power and springiness needed.

A far better technique is to make a sandwich of flat strips of wood (you can find these in the dowel section of most craft shops, or make your own if you have a table saw). Cut the strips into a series of three or four decreasing lengths, and

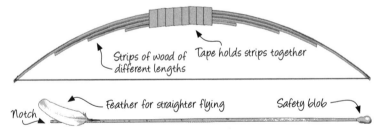

Strips of wood of different lengths   Tape holds strips together

Notch   Feather for straighter flying   Safety blob

stack them on top of each other; bind the center together with tape, as in the diagram above. When you now fix a string to each end, bending the bow so the shorter strips are on the inside, you'll have a strong bow that really works.

Arrows can be made from any straight pieces of dowel or bamboo—twigs from your yard won't be straight enough. Cut a notch in the end for the bow string to slot into, and tape a feather or scrap of paper slightly further down for a flight. Fix a blob of Silly Putty onto the business end: this will provide extra weight to ensure better flight, as well as minimizing damage to windows and corneas.

The indigestion rocket

Would digital photography have taken off so quickly if every Dad knew the fun to be had from those plastic 35mm film containers? With only a drop of water and a fizzing antacid tablet such as Alka-Seltzer you can transform one into a rocket. How come our own Dads didn't tell us this?

Alka-Seltzer and water combine . . .

. . . to fire the film can into the air

An al fresco launch site is most sensible. Pop a tablet into the canister; then, with the lid ready in your hand, drop in a teaspoon of water. In double-quick time, slam the top on, making sure it's sealed, and place the canister upside down on the ground or a table.

Retire a few feet and wait. Ten to 20 seconds later the main part of the canister should shoot 10 feet or so into the air with a satisfying pop, leaving behind a partly dissolved tablet and the lid.

This happens because when the tablet begins to dissolve it creates carbon dioxide. The pressure of this gas builds up inside the canister until the lid pops open. The process is similar to that used by real rockets, although their fuel and aerodynamics are rather more efficient. Unlike NASA's craft, however, the aerodynamics of a film canister can be improved with cardboard fins and nose cone.

If you don't have antacid tablets on hand, you can try other fuel. Baking powder works pretty well, either mixed with water or lemon juice. You can also try antacid powder instead of tablets. Wrapping it in a thin layer of tissue or toilet paper will delay the reaction by a precious second or two.

Different types of film canisters seem to work better than others. Use clear, white ones and you can glimpse the reaction at work. If you no longer have a 35mm camera, ask your local drugstore to hang on to some canisters for you. They only throw them away otherwise.

Next time somebody tells you how great digital photography is, you ask them if they can shoot a flash card 10 feet in the air with just a tablet and some water. That should shut them up.

The spinning helicopter

We all remember collecting sycamore or maple seedpods, throwing them in the air and watching them spiral to the ground. Here's a more impressive version that's easy to make, requires no advanced knowledge of tree identification (see page 54) and can be produced at any time of year.

Begin with any sheet of scrap paper. Cut it into a rectangle in roughly 2:1 proportions—any size will do—and then trim away two smaller rectangles to form a squared-off Y shape (see diagram). Cut down the middle of the thick part, and fold the two "rotors" 90° in opposite directions.

Attach a small weight to the bottom—a paper clip works best—and drop it from a height, such as a kitchen chair or down the stairwell. The paper will spin appealingly as it flutters to earth.

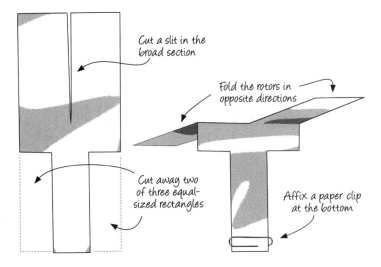

Cut a slit in the broad section

Fold the rotors in opposite directions

Cut away two of three equal-sized rectangles

Affix a paper clip at the bottom

This is a great activity for a group of bored kids on a rainy day: challenge them to vary the size of the paper, length of the rotors and number of paper clips to come up with the "best" design—the one that stays in the air longest.

Do make sure it *is* scrap paper they're using, and not your tax return, child's birth certificate or publisher's royalty checks.

How to make your own kite

While shop-bought kites are certainly fun to use, nothing can compare with the sense of satisfaction you get from making your own out of scrap. This version is made from an ordinary garbage bag. It's the brainchild of Web designer and kite enthusiast Roy Reed, and you can find out more about it and about kite flying on his Web site, www.reeddesign.co.uk.

First, lay your garbage bag out and cut it according to the diagram below. (The darker portion is the section that will become the kite.) The cut-off portion on the left should be cut into 1¼ inch strips, to be used for making the tail.

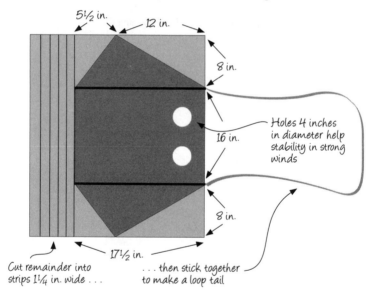

5½ in.

12 in.

8 in.

Holes 4 inches in diameter help stability in strong winds

16 in.

8 in.

17½ in.

Cut remainder into strips 1¼ in. wide . . .

. . . then stick together to make a loop tail

The two holes in the sail (the rectangular, central part) are optional, but help to stabilize the kite when it's really windy. Once you've cut the kite out, lay sticks or dowels along either side of the rectangular central area and tape them in place, then fold up the two edges at 90° to the main body.

You'll need to reinforce the corners of the wings, where the bridle is attached, or it will simply tear out: tape a scrap piece of bin liner over the corners, doubling its

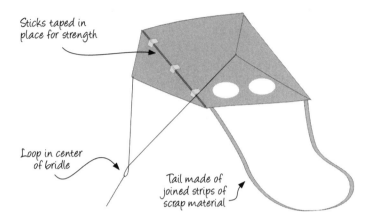

Sticks taped in place for strength

Loop in center of bridle

Tail made of joined strips of scrap material

thickness for extra strength. Tie a nylon line for the bridle to both corners, making a loop at exactly the center point; then tape together all the offcut strips to make the tail (around 3 feet long) and fix it in place beneath the main sail. Like the holes in the sail, the tail isn't strictly necessary, but it does help the kite to fly better.

And that's it—your kite is ready. There's plenty more about kite lines and flying techniques on pages 58–60.

Baked bean can telephones

They don't have to be baked bean cans, of course—any old cans will do (although if they've previously been used for cat food, give them a good wash first or your children will recoil when you kiss them goodnight).

This is such an old staple that it hardly seems worth repeating—until you realize that kids aren't shown how to do this in school anymore, and that for any children brought up on a diet of satellite TV, the Internet and home computers, the idea that any device can transmit your voice without electricity is truly astounding.

Make a hole in the bottom of each of two cans, and thread a length of string (it can be up to 100 feet or so) between the two. You could also try some of that line you cut off your kite when it got stuck in the tree. Tie a knot in each end so that when you pull the string taut, they don't slip out. Talk into one end, while your child listens in the other: Echo Uniform Romeo Echo Kilo Alpha!

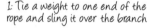

1: Tie a weight to one end of the rope and sling it over the branch

2: Throw the other end over the branch about two feet away

How to hang a garden swing

Swings appeal to kids of all ages, from toddlers who rock gently back and forth to young teenagers who treat them as a cross between an army assault course and a jungle vine.

What puts most Dads off hanging swings is the effort involved: risking life, limb, and pride trying to climb the tree, screwing bolts into the branches or trying to recall knots from Boy Scout days. Here's a much better method that involves neither fixings nor ladders. It can be used to hang a swing from the highest of branches, and can be completed in around ten minutes (depending on your aim).

Make sure you choose a strong, thick branch on a good tree. The branch should be as close to horizontal as you can find, otherwise the swing will veer off to one side. The branch should be in good condition: if it has plenty of leaves at the end, that's fine. If it looks bone dry and sprouts nothing but dead twigs, you may have to rethink.

You need a length of rope roughly three times as long as the height of the branch. A third of this will be cut off later, but you can always find a use for a good piece of rope. Nylon rope is strong, efficient, cheap and ugly; traditional hemp rope looks more attractive but will tend to expand and shrink with the weather. It's

3: Pass the two ends of the rope through the loop on the other side

4: Pull on the rope ends to tug the loop up to the top

your call, and you have to balance aesthetics against practicality. If you do choose nylon rope, make sure it's thick enough for children to get a good grip without cutting their hands.

Begin by tying a weight to one end of the rope—a wooden mallet with a handle is easy to throw. Sling this over the branch (1). It can take a few attempts to get it in the best place, but it's worth the effort of getting it right. Tie the weight to the other end of the rope, and throw this over so there's a gap of around two feet between the two overhangs (2). This gap, which should be at least the width of the swing, is important: again, take the trouble to get it right.

Now take the two ends and pass them through the loop that's hanging over the other side of the branch (3). Pull on the ends, and the loop will raise itself up to the top. When you pull tight, this loop will lock the ropes in position against the branch (4), providing a fixing-free attachment that will be good for years to come.

Swing yourself on each rope in turn to check for strength: if each is strong enough to hold your weight, then the combination of the two should be enough for anything your kids can do to them. Thread the ends through a wooden seat, knot them, and cut off the excess.

The thunderclap

If you're old enough to remember the days (it wasn't *that* long ago) when comics came with free gifts you actually wanted, then you'll experience a nostalgic thrill when you make a thunderclap. It's what we've christened those triangular-shaped toys that make a satisfying bang when you whip them through the air.

The easiest way to make them is to use those "Please Do Not Bend" letter-sized envelopes, with cardboard on the back and a paper front. You've probably tucked a few used ones away for reuse. If you're like us, the chances are you've had them for years, so you may as well use them now.

On the cardboard back of the envelope, mark a triangle the entire bottom width and as tall as it is wide (almost 8½ inches in the case of letter-sized). Cut it out, cutting through the entire envelope. Measurements aren't critical, so don't beat yourself up if you don't have a perfect isosceles triangle.

Unfold the paper triangle. Fold the double triangle of cardboard and paper along the center line, using a ruler or a book to score the cardboard. It should be folded so that the paper stuck to the cardboard is on the *inside*. The paper triangle should then be cut down into a smaller triangle. In our experiments, the optimum height was around two-thirds of the height of the cardboard.

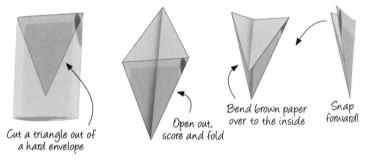

Cut a triangle out of a hard envelope

Open out, score and fold

Bend brown paper over to the inside

Snap forward!

Fold the paper triangle inside the cardboard. Hold the pointed end of the cardboard triangle, slightly open, with the paper triangle toward the ground. Bring your arm down sharply and you should hear a satisfying crack.

You can make bangers from sheets of newspaper or brown paper. But although the noise they make is similar, the nostalgic frisson just isn't the same. It is virtually guaranteed, of course, that the moment you cut up your remaining cardboard envelope you'll need to send something that mustn't be bent.

5 Town and country

IT'S A DANGEROUS PLACE, the countryside. Cows glare menacingly over hedges and deposit booby traps on footpaths. Seemingly shallow puddles turn out to be knee-deep potholes. And vultures gather on telephone wires, waiting for the hapless hiker to collapse with exhaustion.

Worst of all, urbane Dads-about-town are supposed to shed decades of metropolitan sophistication and transform themselves into experienced pastoral guides able to identify trees, start a fire with their bare hands, and predict what the weather will be doing a week from next Thursday.

Urban excursions can be equally fraught. How do you keep children amused during a lengthy shopping trip? How do you make them wait patiently for their meal to arrive, or for you to finish that well-deserved pint?

This chapter is for Dads venturing far from home comforts, TV and the security of their cars. We can't make The Great Outdoors a safe place to visit, but we can make it more bearable.

How to skim stones

Stone skimming, also known as *Ducks and Drakes,* is an ancient diversion which once saw people trying to bounce oyster shells on water. Now they use stones, which no longer restricts them to those months when oysters are in season.

Fortunately for those who aren't natural stone skimmers, a team of French researchers, armed with a mechanical catapult and more money than sense, has investigated the optimum conditions for getting stones to skim on water.

As you might expect, a stone is more likely to skim if it is spinning than one

that isn't: the faster it spins the better. Flicking the stone with your index finger as you release it will increase the speed of rotation. The speedier the stone, the more likely it is to bounce.

When hunting for stones, the flatter and rounder they are, the likelier they are to skim well. If you still find the stones aren't spinning, the French team's earth-shattering discovery is that the perfect angle for a spinning stone to touch the water is 20° (imagine a right angle, halve it, halve it again, shave a tiny bit off and you're there).

For those who feel ready to take on anyone at *Ducks and Drakes,* the World Stone Skimming Championships are held each year at a disused slate quarry on Easdale Island, the smallest permanently inhabited island of the Inner Hebrides, which is off the west coast of Scotland. Although the amateur stone skimmer usually takes pride in the number of "bounces," the Championships value distance instead. If you can't keep a stone going for at least 100 feet, you haven't a chance.

Shaun the sheep

Not many people know that every flock of sheep contains one called "Shaun." Your kids might be skeptical but if you yell "Shaun" out loudly, you are almost certain to be rewarded by at least one sheep turning its head to look at you. That, of course, is Shaun.

I'd rather not be shorn, thank you

Amateur weather forecasting

It's said that townies are now so disconnected from what goes on in the countryside that many kids don't even realize that milk comes from cows. Country folk, on the other hand, are supposed to be so much at one with nature that they can even use it to forecast the weather.

Pine cones, for instance, are said to be an infallible weather indicator. They open out in dry weather and return to their normal shape in wet weather. Amazing. You'd have thought that, by the time you've trudged through a couple of sodden fields to find a pine cone, you'd already have a pretty good idea of how wet it is.

If these jolly rustics aren't studying pine cones, then it's cows. When they sense rain, cows will apparently all troop off to one side of the field and lie down together. Does it work? In Britain it does—it rains so much they're bound to get it right most of the time. But if cows are so good at forecasting weather, how come an enterprising TV channel hasn't signed one up? After all, it would be a lot cheaper than a human forecaster and would almost certainly have better dress sense too.

Whether townie or yokel, if you know somebody who claims they can sense approaching rain through aches in their bones, they might not be talking total rubbish. After all, the weight of the earth's atmosphere is so great that, at sea level, we all—depending on our size—live with ten to twenty tons of pressure squeezing us from all sides.

Bad weather is preceded by a drop in atmospheric pressure—this is the only time you'll hear frogs croak—so it's bound to affect our bodies as well. And that includes Granny's knees, which now seem just as reliable a weather forecaster as pine cones, or most of the "professionals" on TV.

Our fathers used to keep highly polished mahogany barometers, which they would rap with their knuckles at regular intervals. They'd peer for long periods at the arcane markings on the crackled enamel dial before pronouncing with a deafening finality: "Changeable."

Barometers may now be electronic and plastic-cased, but if you're ever called upon to make a prediction, "changeable" is still your safest bet.

Identifying trees by their leaves

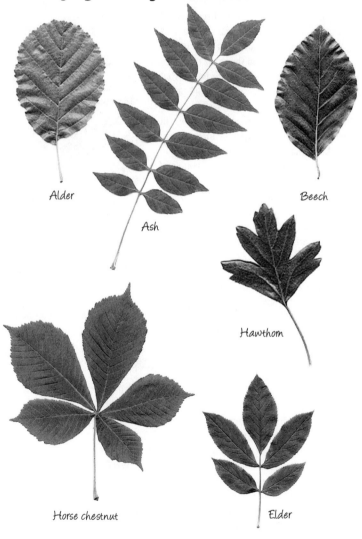

Alder

Ash

Beech

Hawthorn

Horse chestnut

Elder

Hazel

Holly

Oak

Birch

Sycamore

Field Maple

Images courtesy of the Woodland Trust.
More free nature stuff for families at
www.naturedetectives.org.uk

Daisy, daisy . . .

Encouraging children to make daisy chains—another traditional pastime we rarely seem to see anymore—is an excellent way of buying yourself a bit of peace and quiet. When they collect the daisies, they should break off a decent length of stem. The longer they are, the fewer daisies are needed to complete a chain.

Split the stem with a fingernail

Whether you make the chain as you go along or collect a supply of daisies first, the method is the same. Make a hole with the fingernail halfway down the stem, long enough to open up to take another daisy stem but not so long that the stem will split. Push the stem of another daisy through the hole until the flower stops it going any further. Make a hole in the stem of this one, thread another daisy through that, and so on.

You can make necklaces, bracelets, crowns or even garden or table decorations. And if there are no daisies to be found, suggest the children make a dandelion chain instead.

The magic helping hand

When you're out walking, tired kids (or adults) occasionally need a helping hand, particularly when tackling hills. Instead of knocking yourself out by pushing them along or even carrying them, place your hand on what New Agers call the Sacral Triangle. For those whose knowledge of anatomy is less than perfect, this is simply the base of the spine.

You don't need to push, just place your hand there. Without any pressure being applied, it is as if some mysterious force is helping to propel them along.

We know it sounds crazy, rather as if we're extolling the power of pyramids or crystals. But work it does, despite expending no energy. If you don't believe us, go out and try it while we get back to our cold fusion experiments.

How to get out of a maze

Some public mazes are the full monty, with impenetrable walls of hedge, brick or growing corn. Others are floor patterns made of turf, stone, or even water. Kids love mazes and usually charge around them at full pelt.

Dads may prefer to demonstrate their calmness and intellectual superiority. If the maze is of a simple construction, such as at Henry VIII's maze at Hampton Court Palace in England, merely keep one hand next to the wall on that side and turn in that direction at every opportunity. You'll encounter many dead ends but will eventually emerge at the exit.

Unless you're sure of the maze, don't boast to your kids that you can beat them through it. Irritatingly, many modern maze-makers design tricky island mazes with disconnected sections where the one-hand-to-the-wall method dooms you to going in circles. You can trust to logic and common sense to get you through or else find a way to mark each failed route. If you're of a classical bent, you could always pay out thread as you go. If you encounter a ferocious man with a bull's head, though, it's probably best to retire gracefully to the pub, there to think up some really good excuse about what became of the children.

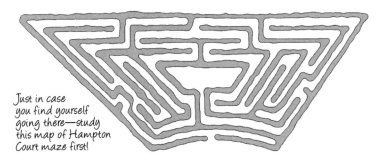

Just in case you find yourself going there—study this map of Hampton Court maze first!

Take aim . . . duck!

Feeding the ducks is a great outdoor occupation for smaller children. But it bores the average Dad silly. Surely this innocent pastime can be given a twist?

The solution is to pick one duck from a flock, and throw the piece of bread so that only *that* duck gets to eat it. It takes both careful aim and diversionary strategies to get it right, and means you'll be playing for as long as your child wants to.

*I've done it! I've done it!
...where's everybody gone?*

How to fly a kite

Number two on the hit parade of Dad images, only just behind chasing a bike yelling, "I won't let go," is Dad trying to get a kite aloft by running backward and falling flat on his arse in the process.

The point of kites is that the wind should do the hard work, not you. Throw a bit of grass or sand up and see which way the wind is blowing. If you're on a hill, a good launching spot is a little way below the peak. Get someone to stand behind the kite and hold it, right way up, facing the wind while you unwind a decent length of line. Take up the tension on the line but don't pull yet.

When the wind picks up, yell to your assistant to let go. Tug the line, and the kite should rise into the air. If the only way to stop it fluttering back down to the ground is to run backward, then there isn't enough wind. If it nosedives into the ground, there's too much. Look at the treetops, ensuring they aren't too close or you can bet that's where your kite will end up. The branches should be moving a little. A wind of five to fifteen mph is suitable for most kites. If you're finding the wind uncomfortable, then so will a standard kite.

As the kite goes up, pull the line to get it to climb to a peak before paying it out again, repeating the process until you're near the end of the line.

Once the kite is safely in the air, you can make it move about the sky by pulling and releasing the line, always being ready to wind the line in gently to keep the kite up if the wind drops. Keep some of the line in reserve. If the kite dives, let the line go slack and it should right itself. If you pull on the line, you'll simply exacerbate the dive.

If the kite doesn't perform properly, try adjusting the angle of the bridle, the bit you attach the line to. Make sure you mark it, though, so you can restore it to the factory-set position if you make a mess of things. In higher winds, move the bridle up toward the nose of the kite. In lighter winds, move it down so the kite is at a more perpendicular angle to the wind.

And if your kite does get stuck up a tree, leave it there. Rather than risk limb, if not life, it is easier to buy another one. If the kids are fond of it, get one that looks the same. Much like guinea pigs, really.

The right kite for the job

These days, there are more kites to choose from than there are models of car and with far more exciting color schemes. It makes sense to buy two or three so you can take advantage of different conditions—kites, that is, not cars.

In light winds, use a light kite or a kite with a large surface area. If the wind is substantial, the kite needs either to be small or vented (with holes in it). Single-line kites can be difficult to fly in heavy winds and might necessitate wearing gloves to avoid burns from the line. It's best to stick to flying in moderate conditions.

The most popular designs for family flying are the diamond (those with a bent horizontal spar tend to fly best) and the triangular deltas. Kites with tails not only look prettier, but are often more stable. Parafoils—like sophisticated windsocks —can be pricier, but fly in a wide variety of conditions.

Different kites may need different strengths of line. Using the wrong weight will harm the kite's performance or could even lose it altogether. Ask for advice from an expert. If you're in a kite (or fishing) store, buy some clips and swivels. The clips go on the end of the flying line and the swivels on the bridle. They will stop the line twisting and save a good deal of time getting the kite ready . . . and putting it away when the kids get bored.

How to fly a stunt kite

If your children enjoy kites, consider adding a stunt kite to your collection. Controlled by two lines rather than one, these are great Dad toys. Pull on the right control and the kite moves to the right. Pull further and it loops the loop to the right. And vice versa.

Needing dependable winds to fly properly, stunt kites are immense fun, swooping through the sky at your will. Get one with a tail that inflates with air and you can make shapes and letters in the air. Start with a robust and inexpensive model while everyone is still in the learning phase.

Stunt kites are hard to get into the air without a helper. After you've assembled one, making doubly sure all the bits are in the right place, unwind both lines, laying them on the ground. Flying with the lines fully extended cuts the chance that they will be uneven, sending the kite into an inescapable death spin. This might damage the kite and will almost certainly take an age to untangle.

As with single-line kites, the helper should stand with their back to the wind and the nose of the kite up. Make certain the control in your right hand is attached to the right of the kite and vice versa. As you launch, pull both lines together and the kite should climb.

Only when the kite is at its peak should you, very gently, pull the kite first one way, then the other. As you become more confident, you can try looping a loop. Remember to bring your hands level again when the kite becomes vertical after the required number of loops. It makes sense to loop the kite an equal number of times the other way to get the lines free again.

Once you become an accomplished stunter, the cool way to land is to fly the kite to one side and touch it down on the ground gently. If you get really cocky, you can even attach several stunt kites together. It looks fantastic, but you really don't want to find yourself with a train of half a dozen kites ready to be brought down and put away, only to discover that your posse of assistants have become bored and wandered off.

FASCINATING FACT

The kite that built a bridge

When they wanted to put a bridge across the Niagara River near the famous falls in the 1840s, they were faced with a serious problem. The water was too dangerous to work in, so how could they span the 800-foot-wide gorge?

Somebody suggested kites and a contest was set up. An American boy, Homan Walsh, won the 10-dollar prize when his kite got caught in a tree on the Canadian side. A light line was attached to his kite string and pulled across. A slightly heavier line was fastened to that and so on, until they eventually got a heavy-duty wire cable across.

That kite line was the beginning of what became, in 1854, the world's first suspension railway bridge.

Starting a fire

Every Dad should be able to build a campfire. Or, at least, be able to show how it would be done if only you'd been lucky enough to have assembled the right combination of leaves, sticks, stones, and weather.

You'll need to gather some dried grass and leaves, placed around a small hollow in a log or the ground. If it's been raining, forget it. You won't have a chance. You then need a fire stick—any straight stick around a foot and a half long will do. This rests on another piece of wood in the assembly of leaves and twigs; the other end is held in place with a stone that also has a slight hollow in it, deep enough to allow the stick to rotate freely. You'll also need a makeshift bow, made by tying a piece of string between two ends of a bendy stick.

With one hand, hold the stick in place by pressing lightly with the stone on the top end. With the other hand, wrap the bow string around the stick once, and then saw back and forth, spinning the stick in the leaves. This method is far more effective—and far easier—than trying to spin the stick between your hands. With any luck (and you'll certainly need some), after a couple of minutes the friction caused will start a small fire in the dried grass.

Don't forget to take a book of matches with you, though, so you can whip it out when no one's looking and start a *real* fire.

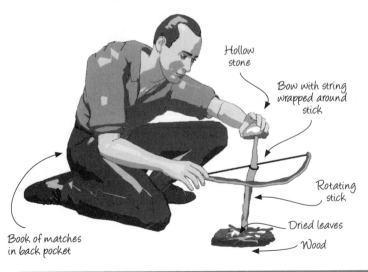

Hollow stone

Bow with string wrapped around stick

Rotating stick

Book of matches in back pocket

Dried leaves

Wood

Bar games

Although pubs, particularly away from the big cities, are generally more welcoming to families than in days gone by, your children may still get bored before their Cokes go flat. You may need to find ways to keep them happily occupied.

If you've come unprepared, ask the staff. The unlikeliest of pubs keep a selection of games behind the bar. Even a pack of cards will suffice.

If not, you may have to resort to that old standby—flipping coasters. This is an essential life skill your children really need to acquire, particularly if they plan on going to university.

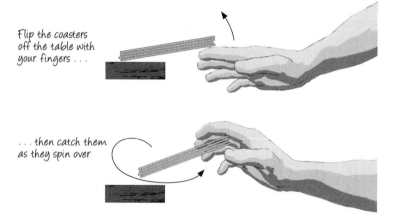

Flip the coasters off the table with your fingers . . .

. . . then catch them as they spin over

A pile of coasters is placed on the table sticking out a little way over the edge. Without touching the table, the back of the hand must be brought up smartly to launch the stack of coasters into the air and then catch them cleanly after they have turned through 180°.

How many can you manage? Six? Eight? Perhaps ten? Don't get too smug. While Britain may struggle to make much of a showing at the Olympics, when it comes to pub sports we're in a league of our own. Dean Gould of Felixstowe holds the current record—208. He can also speed flip: 25 piles of 40 in 45 seconds.

Mr. Gould is a prodigious chap. He holds records for pancake tossing, egg holding, brick flipping, CD flipping, stamp licking, currant eating, grape eating (with plastic spoon), rice eating (with chopsticks), sweet corn eating (with a swizzle stick), dry cream-cracker eating, spaghetti eating, and even meatball eating (both with and without juggling them first). He can also recall the first 1,000 digits of Pi from memory in just over eight minutes.

If you encounter him in a pub, buy him a drink by all means. Just don't make a bet with him.

Flippin' heck

With your arm bent back, place a quarter on your elbow. Bring your hand forward and, palm down, snatch it. Got the hang of that? Now see if you can manage two coins or more. If you drop any, count only those successfully caught.

Just in case you or your brood feel inclined to have a pop at the coin-snatching world record, Dean Gould (yes, him again) holds the current title, for snatching —and this is not a misprint—*328* quarter-sized coins in one grab. It's probably not worth bothering trying to snatch dominoes, either. Dean's been there already.

Dean's kids, presumably so fed up with Dad breaking so many records, decided to have a go too. Amy, 8, and Adam, 11, currently both hold records for hanging from a bar with two hands, while Adam's top dog at heading a football back to a thrower and Amy has no equal at paper-cutting. In ten minutes, she cut an 8x11 inch piece of paper into 1,171 pieces.

Record-breaker Dean Gould demonstrates his coaster-snatching technique, while his daughter Amy shows how to cut a piece of paper into 1,171 pieces

The "Harry Worth"

Back in the 1960s, one of the most popular comedians on British TV was amiable bumbler Harry Worth. He was best known for the opening of his show, imitated at the time by almost every child in the land.

Stopping by a glass-fronted shop, Harry stood sideways in the doorway. Pressing his nose against the glass with only half his body showing, he lifted one arm and leg: the reflection gave the appearance of raising both sets of limbs at the same time.

In the 1960s, this is what passed for cutting-edge comedy in Britain

The gag deserves reviving. It's an excellent way of lifting spirits when you're trudging through town, or waiting in shoe and clothes shops. It's amazing how eager assistants become to speed you on your way when you and the kids are using the store's full-length mirrors for such shenanigans.

Resist the temptation to do "The Full Harry." Donning a drab suit, thick glasses, and a soft felt hat could mean your kids refuse ever to be seen in public with you again.

Put a knot in it

You're sitting at the table in a restaurant waiting for the food to arrive. The kids are getting fractious. If the place is posh enough to provide proper cloth napkins, try challenging your brood to see if they can tie a knot in theirs.

The catch is that they must grasp it at opposite corners and make the knot without letting go. As they twist and contort themselves, trying to do the impossible, your table may well become the object of attention of other diners. Fine. The challenge works even better with an audience.

When the others finally give up and tell you it can't be done, fold your arms with one hand in front of an arm and the other behind. Pick up your napkin at each end with your hands in this position and then pull your arms apart. The napkin will have a knot in it.

6 Are we there yet?

PLANES, TRAINS, AND AUTOMOBILES all test a Dad's ingenuity and entertainment skills to destruction. You may be the best juggler in the neighborhood. You may be the best piggy-back mount west of the Urals. But neither will be a jot of use when you're on the move. You're on your own, with only your wits to help you.

Keeping children occupied on long journeys takes more than iPods, comics, and packets of potato chips. Eventually even the most seasoned adolescent traveler will utter the four words that make every Dad raise his eyes in despair: "Are we there yet?" It isn't the words themselves that are so chilling, but the implication behind them: that the child is now so bored that they are looking to you for entertainment—and woe betide you (and your fellow travelers) if you fail in the task.

In this chapter you'll find car games and plane games to keep young minds amused and active as the miles tick away. From a multitude of diversions which can be used to occupy children, we've chosen those that, in our experience, give the maximum entertainment value for the effort expended.

License plate games

You can relieve the monotony of freeway driving by playing games using the license plates of the cars around you. One of the most popular requires players to find cars from as many different states as possible. The kids can play together or compete against each other.

You can either see who can find the most states in a set period or, if you're on a really long journey, continue until somebody gets a complete set. Unless you want the game to go on forever, however, you might want to exclude Alaska and Hawaii. You can choose whether to include the District of Columbia, Quebec or British Columbia.

Alphabet Search

This is a good game to play in towns or on country roads rather than highways. Look for something you pass beginning with the letter A (such as an airplane, Audi, or even automobile). After they've seen an A, move on to B, and so on, right through the alphabet.

It must be something you pass. While E is indeed for elephant and O is for ostrich, unless you're driving through a zoo you can assume they haven't quite grasped the rules of the game.

A couple of additional pointers. V can be for "vent," that triangular section at the rear of passenger windows that usually won't open (or, if it ever did, the handle's broken off by now). If you're stumped by X it can stand for "crossing," unless you find yourself driving down Chung Cheng Road in Hsin-tien City, Taiwan, where there's a xylophone factory. (Thanks, Google.)

The game can be played in two teams if you're feeling competitive, but it works just as well as a collaborative effort. Consider banning words you've had before, otherwise C for "car" and R for "road" may become a touch repetitive.

Are we there yet?

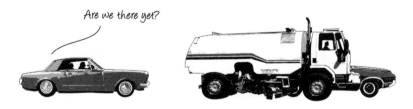

Car Baseball

Each player takes a turn to "bat." They score one run for each car that you pass, or that passes you in the opposite direction. Motorbikes score two; vans four; anything larger, such as a truck or a bus, scores six.

If it's a red car, though, they're out, and play passes to the next player. This keeps going until someone reaches an arbitrary score decided in advance, everyone gets bored or you do finally get there.

You may want to vary scoring methods, depending on whether you're on a busy freeway or a quiet country road. To save later argument, it's worth establishing a few ground rules that can be enforced when the time comes (and believe us, the time will come). No, you don't score 100 if you pass a parking lot full of trucks. Yes, if a car overtakes you, you can score it. Yes, if it's a red car, you're still out. No, if you've stopped at traffic lights, you can't count all the cars that cross your path. And no, I won't break the speed limit to overtake that trailer loaded with shiny new cars.

The Yes/No game

How hard is it to avoid saying "Yes" or "No"? Harder than you might think. This great game is perfect for cars and is suitable for all ages, a great bonus being that adults have no real advantage over kids.

The rules are simple: whoever is "It" has to answer all questions—either randomly or on particular topics—without saying "Yes" or "No." If either word pops out, they lose. It isn't easy when there are so many ways of tripping people up, such as saying, "You said 'Yes' just now"—to which the inevitable response is, "No I didn't!" If they get good at it, you might consider introducing the additional rule that they're not allowed to use improbable, unwieldy answer constructions, such as "I reply in the negative."

Think of Something . . .

If you drive a minivan, or any large car, you'll often find yourself having to entertain a range of children of widely differing ages, whose only common factor is that they're seatbelted directly behind you. *Think of Something* is a game which has served us well, and is as much fun for kids of 4 and 14.

Each child, in turn, is asked to think of an object with a particular characteristic. The game's success depends on Dad varying the question to suit the ability of the child. So young children might be asked to think of something furry, or green, or made of wood; those a little older might be asked to come with something magnetic, or Japanese, or soluble; teenagers might be asked for something Victorian, or contradictory, or made of aluminum.

The older children can answer all the questions in their heads, of course, and it's a great learning tool as younger children aspire to the knowledge of their elders.

Car-Color Bingo

A short, easy game for younger children. Each picks a color, and scores a point for each car of that color you pass. The winner is the first to reach, say, twenty.

If you're the type of Dad who can't bear losing, pick silver. Few children ever do, and it's a surefire winner in these drab, dreary days of automotive anonymity.

Animal, Vegetable, Mineral

The all-time classic car game—also known as *Twenty Questions*, although we don't really see the point in stopping at twenty. Just keep going.

One player thinks of an object, and then defines it as animal (leather, bone, wool and so on as well as real animals), vegetable (any that's grown, such as wood and cotton) or mineral (just about everything else). It can be a combination of these: so

Are we there yet?

a bottle of milk, for example, might be described as "mineral and vegetable, with animal connections"—on the basis that it's made of glass, the contents are made (ultimately) of grass, but with significant animal intervention.

Plastic is tricky, being petroleum-based, as many scientists argue that oil is not a fossil fuel but formed from the remains of plants and animals. Just so long as your children aren't secret subscribers to *Scientific American* magazine, we suggest simply opting for mineral.

The other players then take it in turns to ask suitable questions to try to work out what the object is. Here are a few of the things that might be asked:

Is it man-made?

Is it decorative or functional?

Have we got one?

Is it used inside or outside the house?

Is it bigger than my head? (A much better question than "*Is it big?*")

Have I ever seen one?

Can you eat it?

Is it solid?

Is there just one of them, or lots?

Is it heavier than a car?

Questions like "Does it start with the letter 'T'?" should be discouraged.

The answerer should only reply "Yes," "No" or, in some cases, "I don't know." If you're being kind, you might add a "usually" or "sometimes" if asked whether mud is found in the house. Again, kindness suggests you'd answer "yes, but not only children" if you're asked whether children use CDs. Adults asking imprecise questions should be shown no such mercy.

Whoever gets the answer right gets to pose the next puzzle. With practice, children can come up with some really tricky posers. We struggled for ages with Joe's mineral, bigger than our house, not a building or a mountain, before we discovered it was a cloud.

5-4-3-2-1

Players take it in turns to spot an interesting object, such as a cow, barn or church steeple, out of the window of the car. They then say "Cow!* 5…4…3…2…1" and the other players have to locate, point to and say the name of the object before the countdown has reached 1. Whoever identifies the object first is the next spotter.

If you're feeling competitive, you can add to your score the number the questioner reached when the spotter interrupted the countdown. It's a great inclusive game for the whole family, and has the great advantage of encouraging kids to put down their damn comics and actually look out of the window for a change.

* *Unless the object isn't a cow, of course.*

Counting down the miles

"How fast are we going, Dad?" Pity the child foolish enough to ask this one. For there are tenth-mileposts alongside every Interstate, with larger ones every mile. Watch at the ready, you ask them to count the number of mileposts the car passes in, say, five minutes.

"How many five minutes are there in an hour?" you ask, hoping to get the answer, "Twelve." Multiply the number of mileposts by 12 and you get the car's speed in miles per hour.

We'll be there before you can say . . .

". . . sixteen slimy serpents slithered surreptitiously on the silver sand as they sped silently southward." Or "On Monday morning I made a model of a magical mouse with many mandibles, and mailed it to a man in Missouri."

It takes a few moments' thought on Dad's part to come up with such sentences. It helps if it's alliterative, like the examples above.

Each time your child gets the phrase wrong, you should repeat it (and you should do your best to remember it exactly, as they're certain to pick *you* up on any

mistakes). It's then down to personal ruthlessness: you shouldn't let the children get away with even the tiniest slip as they try to say the exact phrase back to you. But don't point out their mistake; just say they've got it wrong, and repeat the phrase once more for them.

Dad, I feel sick

Are there any words more calculated to jab an icicle of horror into the heart of a freeway-driving Dad who has just passed the last gas station for 45 miles? Suddenly, that phrase from babyhood you thought you'd never hear again—projectile vomiting—returns to haunt you.

The old standby of opening the window does actually help. Even on a freezing day, it's better than the alternative. Also helpful, apparently, is deep, slow breathing. Researchers in the Psychology Department at Pennsylvania State University threw 46 men and women around in a "rotating optokinetic drum," the sort of torture device for which kids happily stand in line for hours at a theme park. Those guinea pigs who did slow, deep breathing before a second session in the drum were much less likely to vomit than those who didn't. So the earlier you can get sickness-prone kids to breathe deeply, the better. Make them desist from reading and get them to look at distant objects out of the window instead.

And if it doesn't work . . . well, that's what plastic bags were invented for.

On planes and boats, you might want to supplement the breathing with medication given long before it becomes necessary. Just as with adults, the very act of taking something may alleviate the problem.

I Spy . . .

You really don't have to play this game. It is tedious in the extreme. Never teach it to your children and, if they know it, ban them from playing it in your presence. If every Dad does the same, we can kill it off in a generation.

Are we there yet?

Games to play on planes

When traveling by plane, the most interesting things are all happening outside, so let the kids grab the window seat. Not only will the view keep them quieter, but you'll be able to see over their heads anyway.

If you can't pre-book decent seats, get to the airport early. Make sure you ask for places that aren't over the wing (obscuring your view) or too close to the toilet (obscuring your nostrils). Windows on planes rarely line up precisely with the seats. If you are allowed to pick your own seats, try to get them slightly behind the window rather than slightly in front. If you don't get a good position, make a note of the best row numbers on the outward journey so you can ask for them on the way back—remembering, of course, that the interesting sights will be on the other side of the plane.

If you're usually subjected to incessant questions as to where you are, what speed you're doing and what height you are, try to fly on one of those airlines that have video screens showing a map and information on the progress of the flight. It's the perfect "Are we there yet?" tool.

If you're truly obsessed with getting the best seats possible, a short visit to www.seatguru.com will give you all the information you need. And when we say all, we mean *all*.

Angles of flight

Cars go forward and backward. Trains usually go forward, even if it doesn't always feel like it. But planes also go up and down and bank from side to side. This means there's a whole game to be played in estimating the plane's angle, and there are several methods of doing this.

The simplest is to half fill a glass or transparent plastic cup with water. For take-off, you can make a simple pointer with suspended paper clips (assuming taking paper clips on planes isn't regarded as an act of terrorism by the time you read this). If it is, some thread with something to weigh it down will do.

Are we there yet?

Going dotty

The *Dot Game* is a splendid time-filler for plane journeys and for waiting in the terminal for your flight to be called. Dads may fancy they have the intellectual advantage, but they are just as likely to make daft mistakes.

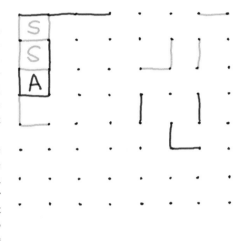

Simply draw a rectangle made up of dots. A square of eight dots by eight is a sensible size. Each player takes turns to connect two dots, the aim being to complete one or more boxes by filling in the last line. That player's initial then goes in the box to be tallied for the final total. Games between Steve and Simon are particularly satisfying, since we both end up believing we've won.

After a player has completed a box, they must then draw another line somewhere. This often leads to strings of boxes being completed in one go, but can then mean the other player also gets a string of boxes to fill in: it's a question of counting the linked boxes to see which offers the best advantage.

What am I drawing?

A pen and pad of paper are invaluable on train and plane journeys. As well as being pressed into service for *Tic-Tac-Toe* and *Hangman*, there's a good collaborative game to be played. Each player takes it in turn to draw an everyday object—a house, a bicycle, a spider, and so on. The other players have to try to guess what they're drawing.

It's a surprisingly even-handed game: older children will try to conceal the finished object by drawing the key elements last (such as the wheels on a bicycle), while younger children may have more trouble simply representing their object, which means it won't become apparent until they've added a lot of detail.

Find the word

Even the most diligent Dad can sometimes find himself on a plane, surrounded by children, with no obvious means of entertaining them.

The one thing you're always sure of finding is an ample supply of in-flight magazines. A fair amount of time can be whiled away with simple word searches —from the more obvious "novelty" and "key ring" to harder-to-find words such as "cheap" and "nasty."

Good words for Hangman

Hangman is a great game for planes, since you're all sitting in a row facing the same way. (It's harder on trains, where some of you will be looking at the paper upside down.)

Everyone plays *Hangman* at some point. It's a common misconception that long words are harder to guess. Of course, it's the other way around: the longer the word, the more chance randomly chosen letters will appear in it, and the more structure will become apparent to let you guess the word.

Short words are much harder, especially if they don't contain any standard vowels. Our favorite is Lynx, but words like Ply, Jinx, Rhythm, Twelfths, and Fjord will certainly keep them guessing.

Do establish right at the outset an agreed construction of gallows and victim so that everyone will get the same number of guesses.

More alphabet fun

Get the children to say, in turn,"A is for . . . ," filling in the gap with a suitable phrase in which all words begin with that letter. Children can make it as silly as they like, so D might be for "Dad's double dumb." The catch is that as each successive letter is introduced, the whole alphabet up to that point must be repeated first. Who will be the first to forget?

Are we there yet?

7 What where who why how?

CURIOSITY MAY HAVE KILLED the cat, but for children it seems to be an energy source. Whatever their first word is, their second will probably be "Why?" And it's usually to Dad that they turn to satisfy this boundless thirst for knowledge. Among their many other necessary skills, Dads have to be walking encyclopedias.

What a cruel trick of nature, therefore, that the arrival of children so often coincides with the atrophying of brain cells in fathers. Nuggets of trivia you've had at your fingertips for years suddenly vanish from your memory and you must suffer the ignominy of having to tell your child that you have no idea what causes tides or how big the Universe is.

Fret no longer. Help is at hand. This chapter will answer only a small fraction of the barrage of questions you will be bombarded with. However, with an expert swerve, you should be able to divert their inquiry into an area in which you can now be an expert. You may not know everything, but you can give the impression you do. Your performance watching *Jeopardy!* should improve too.

Why is the sky blue?

To get to grips with this, two things need to be understood; that white light is actually made up of lots of other colors, and that the sky is not empty.

Gaze upward and you are looking into the Earth's atmosphere, without which life would be impossible. It provides air, water and warmth, while protecting us from meteorites and dangerous radiation. Although it goes on for 300 miles or more, compared to the Earth's size, it is no thicker than the skin on an apple.

The important bit to us is the first ten miles or so. That seemingly empty sky is actually full of water, dust, and a combination of gases (78 percent nitrogen, 21 percent oxygen, and lots of also-rans). Gases, like everything, are full of particles—molecules and atoms. There are 10^{19} of them in just one cubic centimeter of air (around a quarter of a teaspoon).

Sunlight—so-called "white light"—is actually made up of a combination of colors. To prove this to doubting minds, divide a cardboard circle into seven equal segments and color them the colors of the spectrum: red, orange, yellow, green, blue, indigo, and violet. Push a pencil through the center and spin it as quickly as you can between your palms. The colors all merge into white.

When sunlight passes through the atmosphere it smashes into all those particles. Light at the redder, long-wavelength gets through almost unscathed. But at the shorter, bluer, end, it's a different story. Affected 16 times as strongly as red, the atmosphere's particles bat blue light around the sky like a crazy game of celestial Ping-Pong. As a result, wherever we look there's blue light.

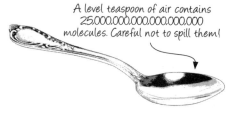

A level teaspoon of air contains 25,000,000,000,000,000,000 molecules. Careful not to spill them!

This scattering not only turns the sky blue, but also makes the sun appear yellow. Out in space, with nothing to scatter light, the sun appears white.

Why are sunsets red?

The sky isn't always blue or we wouldn't have quaint country sayings like, "Red sky at night, the barn's alight."

As the sun sets, the light has to pass through much more of the particle-filled atmosphere. The blue light now gets scattered so much it is absorbed by the atmosphere and we hardly see it at all, while the redder colors are scattered more than before, in the way blue normally is, and so predominate.

Why are clouds white?

The water (and often ice) molecules in clouds are so large that all light colors are scattered equally. Thrown together again the colors recombine and, as we've seen, all the colors together produce white.

If clouds are gray, it could either be because higher clouds are casting shadows on them, or because they are so thick that the sunlight is absorbed higher up, creating a shadow within the cloud.

What does a cloud weigh?

We're glad you asked. Scientist Peggy LeMone of the National Center for Atmospheric Research in Boulder, Colorado, took to wondering about the weight of clouds, presumably after being asked by an inquisitive child.

She worked out that the water vapor in an average-sized cumulus cloud—that's one of the pretty white fluffy ones—weighs 550 tons. If you have trouble envisaging that, she suggests thinking in terms of elephants. As a typical elephant weighs around six tons, that means the water inside a typical cloud weighs the same as 100 elephants.

The obvious next question is: "How does it stay up there?" If clouds were made of elephants, they wouldn't. Those 100 elephants would plummet to earth wearing very surprised expressions and make a sizable mess when they hit the ground. Fortunately for them—and us—the water is in the form of minute particles that are light enough to float on the warmer air rising below the cloud.

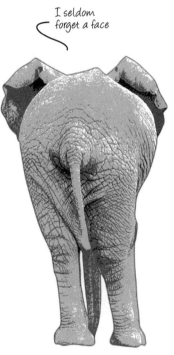

I seldom forget a face

Surprising herself with the figures, LeMone carried on and figured out that the weight of a big storm cloud, one which was 10 times bigger in all dimensions than the cumulus cloud, was a whopping 200,000 elephants.

Why is sea water blue?

Water actually *is* blue. It might look colorless and clear when it's in a glass. But that's because it's only very, very, slightly blue. Put a lot of it together and its true color becomes evident, particularly if the water is deep and clear. Look into a swimming pool, for instance, and the water will probably look a little blue (even if the swimming pool tiles aren't).

If your tap water *does* look blue when it's in a glass, it might be a good idea to check the water tank to see whether anybody has dropped a toilet-freshening tablet into it.

Is every seventh wave a big one?

It's often said that every seventh wave is a whopper, with every *seventh* seventh wave a monster. Although it can be fun to count them as you wave-watch, that's not quite how things work.

Waves are caused by the effect of wind on the surface of the water. The stronger the wind, the higher the waves. Waves don't actually travel toward the shore. That's an optical illusion. In fact, the water simply goes up and down. You can show how waves behave by blowing across the surface of a container of water with something floating on it. This will show that the water doesn't travel horizontally. Flicking a rope will also demonstrate the principle: a wave appears to travel down the rope, but in fact the rope only moves up and down.

In the sea, waves do come in packets of a few smaller waves followed by a few larger ones. The largest of all tend to occur somewhere between the fifth and eighth wave: hence, presumably, the widespread belief that it's every seventh wave that's the biggest.

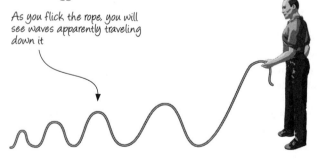

As you flick the rope, you will see waves apparently traveling down it

What causes tides?

The Moon. As the Earth and the Moon dance around each other in the sky, the interaction of their two gravitational fields causes tides—regular rises and falls in the level of the Earth's seas. The Moon's gravity attracts the water nearest to it, while the water on the other side of the Earth also bulges out, since it isn't receiving any gravitational pull at all from the Moon.

There are two cycles of high and low tides each day. During beach holidays, when you have a little more time to contemplate nature in all its beauty and perplexity, you may have wondered why the tides aren't at the same time each day. A little too complicated to go into here (no, we do understand it, really), it's to do with tides being regulated by the moon while our days are determined by the sun (we think). Suffice it to say that the corresponding high (or low) tide the following day will be roughly 45 minutes later.

The strongest tides are spring tides. These have nothing to do with the season but occur when Earth, Sun and Moon are in a line, when the Sun's gravity assists the Moon's. These happen during the full moon and the new moon.

During quarter moons, the Moon and Sun are perpendicular to each other, so we get weaker—or Neap—tides.

How far away is the horizon?

Depends how tall you are. Seriously. It does. The horizon is simply the physical manifestation of the curvature of the earth. That's why ships seen disappearing over the horizon vanish bit by bit. So the higher up you are, the further you'll be able to see.

Someone with eyes 4 feet from the ground will be able to see 2.6 miles. Five and a half feet and it will be 3 miles. Stand on a cliff so your eyes are 60 feet up and the horizon will be 10 miles away.

There's a way to work it out, since you asked. Multiply the height of the eyes (in feet) by 1.74. The square root of this will give you the distance to the horizon in miles. If you want it in kilometers then use centimeters for the eye height and multiply by 0.15 before taking the square root.

Incidentally, it's an interesting fact that the horizon is always, always, *always* at the same level as your eyes: you stare horizontally to look at it. It doesn't matter if you're standing up, sitting down or looking out of a high window. It's a key rule in perspective drawing, but it's very surprising until you try it out!

How many colors are there in a rainbow?

Did you say "Seven?" Go to the back of the class. Even if you have a physics textbook that says that it's seven, we don't care—it's wrong.

There's an indeterminate number of colors, just as in the spectrum. Red doesn't suddenly become orange, nor yellow turn green at some precise point. On the contrary, the colors blend gradually into one another. Try looking at the business side of a CD in sunshine or under bright light, or reflect it onto paper: you'll see plenty of colorful "rainbows" as the light hits the disc's ridges.

FASCINATING FACT

People will often talk about rainbows as if they contain every color there is. This is nonsense, of course. Try looking for brown, white, black, gray, or such colors as silver and gold. They're simply not there.

It's all Sir Isaac Newton's fault. He knew that there were, effectively, an infinite number of colors in the rainbow, but for the sake of convenience he split them into seven. Through everybody else's sloth, idleness and sloppy thinking, this has since become the norm. Nature is a source of infinite wonder. It would be depressing beyond belief if there really were fewer colors in the rainbow than there are in a bathroom catalog.

What causes rainbows?

As we've seen, sunlight actually consists of lots of colors. A rainbow is nature's prism, turning white light back into its constituent parts. For a rainbow to appear, the sun needs to be behind the observer and low in the sky, which is why they usually occur in late afternoon. The bow will be opposite the sun when it is raining or has just rained. The mist of water droplets in a waterfall is another possible source of rainbow sightings.

As sunlight enters the raindrops it is bent, then reflected from the back of the raindrop and bent again as it reemerges from the front. But each color is bent to a slightly different degree: red is bent at a $42°$ angle and violet at $40°$, with all the intermediate colors sandwiched in between.

If you see a double rainbow, it simply means that those droplets have reflected the light inside twice.

A rainbow is really a circle, but the horizon cuts off the bottom half. Complete circular rainbows are, however, occasionally visible from the air.

You can only see rainbows from one side. This is simply demonstrated on a sunny day by making your own rainbow with a garden hose set to produce a fine spray. With the sun behind you, the rainbow will be visible to you but not to but someone the other side of the water, facing the sun.

A good way of showing how water can split up light is to fill a glass or jar with water and place it on an outside table on a sunny day so that almost half of it is off the table. Place a sheet of paper on the ground so the Sun shines through the glass and creates a rainbow on the paper.

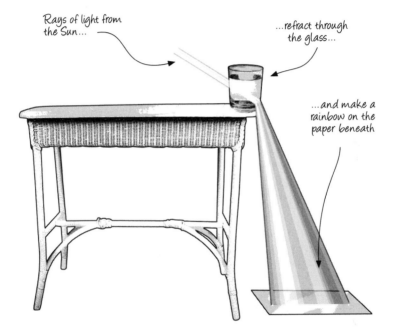

Rays of light from the Sun...

...refract through the glass...

...and make a rainbow on the paper beneath

Despite the legends, there really is no pot of gold at the end of the rainbow. If you move toward a rainbow, it will simply move ahead of you. It's not that we've looked for the gold or anything daft like that. That would be an utterly ridiculous waste of an afternoon, involving such pathetically stupid things as driving a family car through grotesquely wet fields, getting stuck in the mud, arguing with an irate farmer and having to pay him a small fortune to pull us out with a tractor. That's why we'd never be so stupid as to go looking for the pot of gold in the first place. It doesn't exist. Believe us. It really doesn't.

How does a flying buttress work?

Flying buttresses—those pillars of masonry that suddenly lurch over at the top to rest against the outside walls of cathedrals—are almost unique among the arcana of ecclesiastical architecture: not only can we remember their name, but they inspire giggles among younger fans of *The Simpsons*. But what do they do?

For a great practical demonstration, make your child stand with his arms leaning forward at a 45° angle. Explain that he's the wall of the cathedral, and his arms are the roof. Then go on to say that, because of all the lead in church roofs, there's a tremendous weight pressing down from above: at the same time, push on his outstretched arms. He'll naturally move one leg back to steady himself, which is exactly what you want to happen: point to the leg, and tell him: *"That's a flying buttress."*

Your child's body is the wall of the cathedral and his arms are the roof

As you press down on the roof, he puts his leg back to steady himself—and that's what a flying buttress does

Where do babies come from?

Er . . . ask your mother.

She said I should ask you.

I'm busy right now, ask me tomorrow.

No, really, where do babies come from?

Sooner or later, you may have to tackle this one head-on. The standard technique is to fold your newspaper, take a deep breath, and wonder where to start. What you should be doing is wondering where to stop.

Too often, parents can overwhelm their children with information they didn't ask for, aren't ready for, and can't cope with all in one go. Explaining obstetrics in full gynecological detail is as bad as trying to shut them up with drivel about birds, bees and storks. The entire truth is too startling and too downright implausible for a single conversation.

A better approach is to give just enough information to answer the immediate question and no more. Don't try to fill their heads with details they're too young to assimilate. Let them come back to you, in their own time, with follow-up questions once they've processed what you've already told them.

A typical question-and-answer session, which may be spaced over several weeks, might go like this:

Where do babies come from?
They come from inside Mummy's tummy.
How do they get out?
The baby pushes itself out when it's grown big enough.
Where do they come out?
There's a special opening that expands to let the baby out. It's sometimes quite difficult, which is why Mummy needs a doctor to help the baby be born.
How do they get in there?
A tiny seed from Daddy is planted inside Mummy's tummy. It starts off really tiny, so small you can't see it. In nine months it grows into a baby, just like a plant grows from a seed.
How does the seed get in there?
Er . . . ask your mother.

How do planes fly?

They're big. They're heavy. Their wings don't flap. Just how do those metal monsters stay up there? The usual explanation invokes the Bernoulli Effect. This says that air will flow more quickly over the upper, curved section of a wing than the flat underside. A faster flow of air reduces the pressure, giving the wing lift.

What will happen when your child blows between the Ping-Pong balls?

There are some great experiments to illustrate this. Cut a 2-inch strip lengthways from a piece of paper. Hold it on your lower lip and blow straight ahead. The sheet of paper will rise to the horizontal, even with a paper clip attached.

Suspend a couple of Ping-Pong balls or balloons from lengths of cotton or string, so that they are level and a short distance apart. Ask a child what they'd expect to happen if they blew between the gap. They'll usually expect the balls or balloons to move apart. But in fact they come together, the faster airflow resulting in a reduction in pressure.

Hold a funnel upside down—the cut-off top of a water bottle will do. Blow into the narrow end while holding a Ping-Pong ball inside it. As long as you keep blowing, the ball won't fall out because the faster-flowing air—where the pressure is lower —is above it. Hold the ball in the palm of your hand, blow hard, and, amazingly, the ball will be sucked up into the funnel.

FASCINATING FACT

The very first flight, in 1903, by the Wright Brothers, lasted only 12 seconds, the plane traveling 120 feet. The Wright Flyer could have made the entire trip within the length of a modern jumbo jet.

Cut a straw in half and hold it in a glass of water. Blow air hard through a straw held horizontally at the top of the vertical straw. After a little trial and error, the decrease in air pressure at the junction of the two straws should create a spray of atomized water.

Point a hair dryer upward and place a Ping-Pong ball in the stream of air. It will bounce round in the airstream. You can even point the dryer away from the vertical and the ball will stay trapped in the faster air current. Try it with a balloon. Try it with both. If the kids somehow think it's because of the hot air rising, turn the heating element off. You can do the same experiment with one of those bendy straws, the short bit pointing upward, and a Ping-Pong ball.

The standard explanation of how a jumbo jet, weighing nearly 400 tons, flies is that it accelerates to over 150 mph on the runway, at which point the air flowing over the wings is traveling so much faster than the air below the wing that sufficient lift is generated to suck the plane off the ground and keep it there. This is, in fact, complete nonsense.

You can keep a balloon aloft, and steer it around, using an ordinary hair dryer

So how do planes really fly, then?

The Bernoulli Effect is the standard way of explaining how powered flight is possible. It's used in schools, colleges and textbooks. It's great fun to demonstrate. It's also wrong, massively so, when people claim that the air going the longer route over the curved upper wing has to rush to "catch up" with the air beneath it.

It's nonsense. Ask yourself—or prepare to be asked by an alert child—how the Wright Brothers could fly when the wings of the Wright Flyer were flat, not curved, just like a paper dart? How does that fly? And how can a plane fly upside-down when the curved side is toward the ground?

Newton is the key. His Third Law of Motion tells us that, for each action, there's an equal and opposite reaction. Wings are tilted backward or have a tilted trailing edge. As a plane is propelled forward, the wing forces the air beneath it downward. In reaction, the air pushes the wing upward, providing lift. This effect is most obvious with a helicopter. Its rotors are thin, quickly revolving "wings."

Hold a piece of paper down on a table and blow on one of the shorter edges. It will flap about. Crease it a third of the way down and bend that edge up. Now hold it and blow again. The leading edge will rise up. That's how planes can fly. They are effectively "surfing" through the sky. Bernoulli does contribute, because the curvature of the wing improves the lift efficiency. But it's not the whole story.

How do birds fly?

A bird's grace and agility make all our high-tech planes look positively elephantine. It doesn't need a long runway—not when it can land on a target as tiny as a telephone wire.

When gliding, a bird's outstretched wings are angled slightly downward, increasing air pressure below the wings and reducing it above. This gives the bird lift as it moves through the air. If there are warm air currents, called thermals around, it can seek them out and use them to soar to higher levels, just as glider pilots do.

When a bird flaps its wings, on the downstroke it deflects air backward to give it forward thrust. On the upstroke, it partially folds its wings to reduce drag, much in the way that somebody swimming the breast stroke does while they're preparing for their next scoop.

I've caught a fish!

Whoops

Birds are incredibly efficient flying machines. To change direction, they can flap their wings at different rates, as well as tilting and changing the shape of their wings and tail, thus simulating the complexities of the flaps, ailerons, rudders and elevators on planes.

A bird's bones are hollow. If they weren't, it would be too heavy to fly. This is the case with penguins, whose ancestors did fly. But their bones, which are now solid, make it easier for them to swim and dive underwater for fish.

Why is the sea salty?

Although river water tastes fresh (assuming you're high enough up in the hills so that no chemicals or other pollutants have yet washed into it), the water you're drinking actually contains small quantities of mineral salts from rocks and soil which it carries into the sea.

As sea water evaporates, the salt remains behind. Over the years and millennia, sea water gets saltier and saltier. One cubic foot of sea water contains, on average, 2.2 pounds of salt. Ninety-seven percent of all the water on Earth is salty, with only 3 percent fresh (and two-thirds of that is frozen in ice sheets and glaciers).

The saltiest water is in the Red Sea and the Persian Gulf, where there's little fresh water input but high evaporation because of the high temperatures. The Dead Sea in Israel is saltier, at 33 percent, but it's a lake, not a real sea. At 1,300 feet below sea level, it's also the lowest spot on the surface of the Earth.

Interestingly, when ice forms from sea water, the salt is forced out and sinks. Eskimos and explorers can get drinking water just from melting the ice.

Is it worth runnin' in the rain?

If it's raining, will you get more or less wet if you run through it? Scientists with too much time on their hands have debated this periodically (i.e., in learned periodicals) over the years. But it wasn't until 1997 that we got a definitive answer when two meteorologists, Dr. Thomas Peterson and Dr. Trevor Wallis, decided that there was only one way to know for sure.

Marking out a 100-meter track behind their office, they dressed in identical sweatshirts, hats and trousers and sat down to wait for rain. Being meteorologists at the United States National Climatic Data Center in North Carolina, presumably they had a pretty good idea how long they'd have to wait.

When the rain came, out they went. Dr. Wallis ran down the track at 9 mph and Dr. Peterson ambled along at 3 mph. While Dr. Wallis's clothes weighed 130 grams more, the slower Dr. Peterson's clothes gained 217 grams. In other words, if you dawdle in the rain you'll get almost twice as wet.

Further research found the difference to be most marked in heavy rain in windy weather. In light rain it matters much less whether you walk or run.

As for knowing whether it's going to rain or not, the learned Professor Murphy, whose Law holds true in so many walks of life, found that it usually happens when you don't have your umbrella or raincoat with you.

What causes thunder and lightning?

Much like sparks resulting from static electricity (see page 10), lightning is caused when the electrical charges in a cloud separate, with negative charges forming at the bottom of the cloud. These repel the negative charges on the ground, resulting in an overall positive charge at the surface.

As air is a bad conductor of electricity, these opposite charges keep building up until the resistance of the air is suddenly overcome, a circuit is completed and the negative charge finds a way to the ground. A single lightning strike may carry a charge of 100 million volts or more, compared to the 120 volts of our electrical appliances. The temperature in a lightning bolt is 50,000°F—five times as hot as the surface of the Sun. Thunder is caused by lightning instantaneously heating the air, which expands explosively. If you blow up a paper bag and burst it, you get an idea how this happens.

The forked lightning that so impresses us actually travels *up*, not down. It happens too quickly for us to see, but there are actually two strikes for each fork of lightning. The leader coming down from the cloud is like a feeler: a short way from the ground, it attracts a return charge, suddenly connecting ground and cloud.

How far away is a thunderstorm?

In the movie, thunder is heard the instant lightning flashes. If this happened in a real storm, we'd be in danger of being struck by lightning.

Although the flash of lightning reaches our eyes more or less instantly, sound takes longer to get to us. The speed of sound is about 760 miles an hour, or a fifth of a mile in a second. Start counting the seconds from the flash to the roll of thunder. Saying "Mississippi One, Mississippi Two" pretty much ensures you're counting in seconds, even if you're not sure how to spell Mississippi. Divide the number of seconds by five and that's how many miles away the storm is.

You've probably been taught that one second equals one mile. It's a lie! That lightning is much closer than you thought!

What should you do in a thunderstorm?

Stay indoors. It's the safest place.

If you are caught outside, remember that lightning takes the easiest path to ground. That's why tall buildings are struck more often than short ones. Get off

Try to stay away from tall objects, especially tall metal objects filled with rocket fuel. PHOTO: NASA

high ground and keep as low as you can, crouching or kneeling if you can't find any hollows.

Get rid of anything metal and don't stand under or near trees, lampposts or telephone poles. Don't shelter in a cave, stay clear of water and keep your distance from other people.

It's a myth that rubber-soled shoes or rubber tires provide protection. They don't, so don't ride a bike. A car is a pretty safe place as its metal shell will conduct electricity better than you, but keep the windows up and don't touch any metal parts. Commercial airliners are not in much danger in a storm. While it may seem frightening—and bumpy —if you experience it first-hand, most planes are struck once or twice a year. The metal in the fuselage conducts the current around it and away, much like in a car.

Indoors, don't use electrical equipment, particularly those old-fashioned phones that plug into the wall. Avoid water as it's a great conductor of electricity. So no baths or showers. Don't wash your hands or do the dishes, and stay off the toilet. Even kings can die on the throne.

Despite the saying, lightning *can* strike twice in the same place. The Empire State Building gets 100 lightning strikes every year.

Why is it colder the further north you go from the equator?

The wrong answer is that, because it's a globe, the Earth's northern latitudes are further away from the Sun. The difference in distance is insignificant.

Instead, it's to do with the angle of the Sun's rays. The further north you go, the more obliquely they strike the Earth. The sunlight is spread over a greater area, leading to lower temperatures. You can demonstrate this most easily by shining a flashlight onto a piece of paper. It's easy to see that if the angle is slanted then the light (and heat) are being distributed over a bigger area than if the flashlight shines directly onto the paper.

Seasons are also unconnected with the Earth's distance from the Sun. Oddly enough for those of us in the northern hemisphere, the Earth is closest to the Sun at the beginning of January, the middle of winter. Seasons occur because the axis around which the Earth rotates every day is tilted. As the Earth takes its annual tour around the Sun, if the northern part of the globe is tilted toward the Sun then it's summer; the Sun's rays strike more directly and the days are longer. The opposite applies in winter, and in the southern hemisphere.

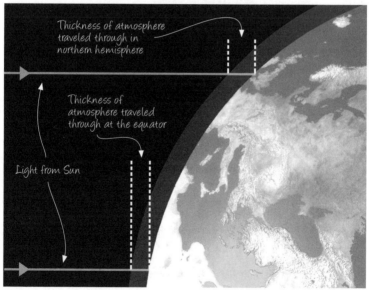

Why do we have leap years?

Although we think of the Earth going around the Sun once a year, in fact it takes 365 days, 5 hours, 48 minutes, and 46 seconds. If nothing was done about that extra quarter of a day each year, our calendars would soon get out of kilter with the solar calendar, which determines our seasons. Then Christmas really would get earlier every year.

So a day is added to our calendars every four years, giving February 29 days rather than 28. If we did nothing, within a few centuries Christmas would be in the middle of summer.

But this isn't quite enough. If we left it at that, we'd gain another day every 128 years. By 1582, when Pope Gregory put things right, we were 10 days adrift. The new, Gregorian, calendar not only leapt ahead those 10 days; it also avoided future minor drifting by skipping leap years in three out of every four century years. So 1700, 1800 and 1900 weren't leap years, though 2000 was.

How much does the Earth weigh?

Nothing. Seriously. Weight depends on gravity and there is none in outer space.

However, the Earth's *mass*, which doesn't depend on gravity, is 6 sextillion metric tons; that's 6×10^{21} metric tons (6,000,000,000,000,000,000,000 metric tons).

What's more, the Earth is gaining weight, at the rate of 40,000 metric tons each year. It's the result of tons of dust and micrometeorites entering the atmosphere every day.

Is it possible to dig right through the Earth?

No. Sorry, but there it is. So you might as well put your spade back in the shed and eat your packed lunch now. You'll never get there.

The deepest hole ever dug is around 7.5 miles deep. It's called Kola SG-3, and was drilled by geophysicists in northern Russia between 1970 and 1989. That's certainly a deep hole, but the distance from the surface to the center of the Earth is nearly 4,000 miles—so even after nineteen years of digging, Kola barely scratches the surface.

If the Kola hole were the thickness of one page of this book, you'd have to drill through the equivalent of eleven copies to get all the way through. (Feel free to buy another ten copies to try this.)

How many moons does the Earth have?

Calling that thing we can see in the night sky "The Moon" could turn out to be something of a misnomer.

In 1986, a second moon was discovered. It's only 3 miles across and, strictly speaking, it's a "co-orbital Near-Earth Asteroid." Just like the Earth and the Moon, it takes a year to go around the Sun, although its path is hugely eccentric from the Earth's point of view, resembling the outline of a horseshoe. Its orbit passes Venus, almost gets to Mercury and then turns back and nearly gets to Mars before heading back again. It's called 3753 Cruithne (pronounced "Croo-EEN-ya"), named after the Celtic tribe better known as Picts.

The closest it gets to us is 10 million miles, 40 times the main Moon's distance. But Cruithne does share Earth's orbit around the Sun. It might not be what you or I would call a moon of ours, but lots of astronomers do.

In September 2002, there was much excitement when an amateur astronomer from Arizona found a small object in a perfect 50-day orbit around the Earth. Thought to be a third moon, it was named J002E2. Then, to everyone's embarrassment, they realized it was *Apollo 12*'s abandoned 3rd-stage booster. Oops!

Some argue that a subsequently-discovered Near-Earth Asteroid called 2002AA29 is a third moon. This one's only 330 feet across and visits the Earth just once every 95 years, the last time in January 2003. So it's really a part-time moon or quasi-satellite.

Perhaps that's just as well for the poets. They might be able to find a rhyme for Cruithne, but they'd have a heck of a job with 2002AA29.

Is the Moon made of green cheese?

In 1546 English dramatist John Heywood jotted down umpteen "proverbes" for posterity, including one that "the moon is made of a greene cheese."

Fortunately for those who don't care for four-and-a-half-billion-year-old cheese, it was Moon rocks, rather than cheese, that the astronauts brought back from the Moon. The idea still persists though.

Oddly, though, Moon rocks are only about a quarter as dense as the rocks of Earth. Their density is far closer to . . . *cheese*! By transmitting shock waves through Moon rocks and assorted Earthly cheeses, scientists found that while Basalt 100017 from the Moon has a seismic velocity of 1.84 km/sec, Vermont Cheddar has a seismic velocity of 1.72 km/sec.

What are the phases of the Moon?

The Moon is unusual in that its rotational and orbital speeds are identical—which is why it always presents the same face toward us. The Moon turns both around its axis and around the Earth once every 27.32166 days.

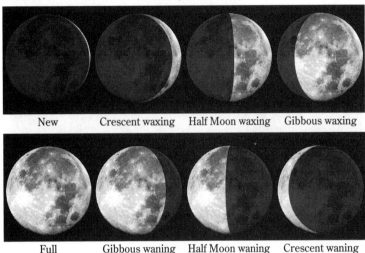

| New | Crescent waxing | Half Moon waxing | Gibbous waxing |

| Full | Gibbous waning | Half Moon waning | Crescent waning |

Is there a man in the Moon?

When the Moon is relatively full, it's easy to imagine that you can see a man's face up there, mouth gaping wide with astonishment.

The eyes are in fact two lunar "seas," Mare Imbrium and Mare Serenitatis, and the mouth is Mare Nubium. Though named as seas by ancient astronomers, these are actually just large dark plains of volcanic rock.

The ancients were keen on trying to find recognizable shapes up in the heavens. But different people saw different things. Other cultures, for instance, didn't see a man in the Moon at all, but things as varied as a hare, a buffalo, a woman and even a kissing couple.

Twelve real men have stood on the Moon. Neil Armstrong of *Apollo 11* was the first on July 20, 1969, and Gene Cernan of *Apollo 17* the last on December 14, 1972.

Spot the difference

Smooth, slimy skin

Rough, lumpy skin

Large back legs for jumping

Short back legs for walking (toads don't jump)

Frog

Toad

One hump

Two humps

Dromedary

Camel

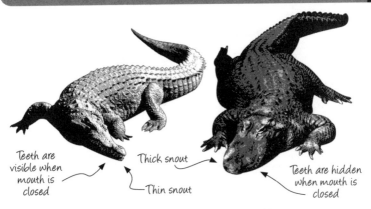

Teeth are visible when mouth is closed

Thick snout

Thin snout

Teeth are hidden when mouth is closed

Crocodile

Alligator

12 feet high

Big ears

Small ears

9 feet high

African

Indian

Fluffy flying teddy bear that makes honey and only stings you when it really has to

Vicious stinger that was a tax inspector in a previous life

Bee

Wasp

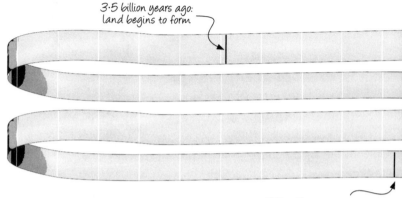

3.5 billion years ago:
land begins to form

550 million years ago:
life starts on Earth

The history of the Earth . . . in a roll of toilet paper

Although the Earth is 4.5 billion years old, human beings in a halfway recognizable form have only been around for, at the most, about 200,000 years. It's pretty hard to get kids' minds (or even adults) to grasp just how minuscule a proportion this is. Unless, that is, you unwind an entire roll of toilet paper.

You may not be as sweet as that mischievous puppy in the commercials, but you can bet that you'll have your kids' attention when you begin rolling out the paper. It's unlikely you'll have enough room to keep going in a straight line. It doesn't matter. Go in and out of rooms, and up and down the stairs. Let the kids dictate where it goes. Try to arrange it so the last few feet run straight and true. (Keep the tube for The Hole in the Hand; see page 13.)

Grab a tape measure and check the length of the roll on the pack. If yours is 100 feet long, as our well-known brand was, then each foot will represent 1 percent of Earth's history, or 45 million years. (You may have to make adjustments if you're using an inferior brand.) Find a way to mark the paper, either directly or on something you can attach to it. Explain that the beginning of the roll is when the Earth was formed, along with the Sun and the rest of the Solar System, around 4,500 million years ago.

Assuming your pace is roughly three feet, follow the roll for seven strides. Make a mark and explain that at this point, 3.5 billion years ago, land began to form and the first, very primitive life appeared in Earth's oceans.

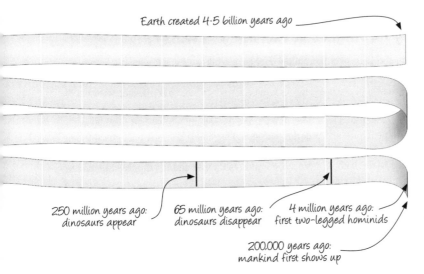

Earth created 4.5 billion years ago

250 million years ago: dinosaurs appear

65 million years ago: dinosaurs disappear

4 million years ago: first two-legged hominids

200,000 years ago: mankind first shows up

You need to go another 66 feet, or 22 paces, before you can stop and make another mark. Here, 550 million years ago, life really got going in earnest, with an abundance of plant and animal species. The earliest fossils found date from this time. No sign of mankind yet, though.

March on until you near the end of the roll. Five and a half feet before it runs out, you should mark the point where, 250 million years ago, the first dinosaurs appeared on Earth.

Seventeen inches from the end, you can show where, 65 million years ago, a giant asteroid wiped out 70 percent of all living things on the planet, including the dinosaurs. (Probably—the scientists are still arguing over that one.)

The first two-legged hominids, where we began to become distinct from our ape ancestors, didn't make their appearance until around 4 million years ago. This, your audience should be amazed to discover, occurred on the very last inch of the roll.

Homo sapiens, the species that we now call mankind, first appeared 200,000 years ago. That's just 0.05 inches away from the end of the roll, too minute a gap to mark, except with a line across the very end bit of the paper. You'd need a magnifying glass to see the start of recorded history 10,000 years ago and even an incredibly powerful microscope wouldn't find the spot that marks when you or your kids were born.

Why do fingers get wrinkly in water?

Stay in the bath or a swimming pool for a while and you'll notice your fingers getting wrinkly. This happens because our skin is lubricated and protected by an oil called sebum produced by our bodies. It's why water runs off when we wash or get caught in the rain.

Stay in water for a long time, though, and the sebum gets washed away, allowing water to penetrate and waterlog our skin. Our hands and feet have the thickest skin and so absorb most water, getting wrinkly, much like the pages of a book dropped in the bath. Elsewhere, our skin is thinner and too tightly stretched to make much difference.

How do fireworks work?

There are two ways of getting fireworks into the air. A rocket has a lower chamber that contains gunpowder, also known as black powder. As it burns, it produces hot gases that escape through a small hole, propelling the firework skyward. Other aerial fireworks are launched from a mortar tube where the explosion of a lift charge fires the firework up to 1,000 feet into the air.

Controlled by a time-delay fuse, the business end of the firework is designed to go off when the firework reaches its maximum height. Pellets of chemicals packed into the firework burn in an enclosed space. The pressure builds until the firework blows up, producing a bang which ignites and scatters the so-called stars, which work much like colored sparklers.

The color of the stars is determined by the metals used. Barium nitrate produces a green effect, strontium is red, sodium sulphate is yellow, magnesium and aluminum are white, carbon is orange, and copper sulphate is blue.

FASCINATING FACT

Many fireworks are still made by hand—*very* carefully. They're so dangerous that even a sharp knock can detonate a star. The danger of sparks from static electricity is such that firework makers are compelled to wear cotton, right down to their underwear.

8 Number crunching

ALL KIDS LOVE NUMBERS. Ever since the first cave kid learned to tot up the number of mammoth bones in his primordial soup, they've been counting everything in sight. Comparing, cataloguing, and enumerating physical objects has been a favorite pastime for millennia.

This can be a problem for the unprepared Dad. Which *is* taller, the Statue of Liberty or the largest of the Pyramids? Does your car weigh more than an elephant? How big is the Earth? How many hairs are there on your head?

Even in a book of this size (total page area: 65 square feet) we (combined height of authors: 11 feet 9 inches) can't hope to include every fact your child might demand of you. But there should still be enough facts here to keep them going from Time Immemorial (1189, a legal term meaning "dating from before the reign of King Richard I") to the end of the world (December 23, 2012, according to the ancient Mayan calendar).

How much did Manhattan cost?

When Dutch merchant Peter Minuit bought the island of Manhattan from the Algonquins in 1626, he paid them in trinkets worth $24. But how much is $24 in today's currency?

We've compiled the table on the facing page from data supplied to us by the Bank of England. To use it, simply multiply the figure shown for each year (or decade, before 1900) to get the value of any sum today.

If we date Minuit's purchase to 1620 we get a figure of 106 from the table opposite. Multiplying this by our $24 gives us $2,544. Even in today's money, it's something of a bargain. But perhaps they weren't taken advantage of after all: recent research by economists shows that, if the Algonquins had invested it at compound interest, they'd now have enough to buy it back again.

So next time your kids' grandmother tells them that she earned $10 a week at her first typing job in 1948, a glance at the table (and a multiplication of 25.5 by that $10) will give an equivalent wage of $255 today—not too bad for a 17-year-old girl's first earned income, especially when you think that her bus ride to work only cost a nickel. Oh, hang on a minute . . .

Useful dates in US history

1492	Columbus sets sail	1908	The Model T is introduced
1620	Pilgrims land at Plymouth	1912	The *Titanic* sinks
1621	First Thanksgiving	1920	Women get the right to vote
1732	Benjamin Franklin establishes first circulating library	1939	World War II starts
		1941	Pearl Harbor attacked
1775	Paul Revere's Midnight Ride	1963	President John F. Kennedy assassinated
1776	Declaration of Independence		
1789	George Washington becomes first president	1964	Civil Rights Act
		1965	Vietnam War starts
1803	Lewis and Clark Expedition	1968	Martin Luther King Jr. assassinated
1838	Underground Railroad organized		
		1969	Neil Armstrong walks on the Moon
1863	Gettysburg Address		
1865	President Abraham Lincoln assassinated	1974	President Richard Nixon resigns
1876	Invention of telephone	1986	Space shuttle *Challenger* explosion
1896	First moving picture shown		
1903	First powered flight	1989	Berlin Wall torn down

Multiply any historical amount of money by the figure listed next to that year in the table to calculate how much it's worth now (see facing page).

2006 ......1.00	1972 ....9.3	1938 ......35.9	1904 ......62.9	**1600** 143
2005 ......1.03	1971 ....9.9	1937 ......35.9	1903 ......62.9	1590 168
2004 ......1.06	**1970** 10.9	1936 ......38.0	1902 ......62.9	1580 201
2003 ......1.10	1969 ......11.6	1935 ......38.7	1901 ......64.9	1570 183
2002 ......1.12	1968 ......12.2	1934 ......39.5	**1900** 64.9	1560 224
2001 ......1.15	1967 ......12.7	1933 ......40.3	1890 ......62.9	1550 335
2000 ......1.17	1966 ......13.1	1932 ......38.7	1880 ......53.0	1540 335
1999 ......1.20	1965 ......13.6	1931 ......38.0	1870 ......50.3	1530 403
1998 ......1.23	1964 ......14.3	**1930** 35.3	1860 ......51.6	1520 503
1997 ......1.26	1963 ......14.7	1929 ......34.1	1850 ......57.5	1510 503
1996 ......1.30	1962 ......15.0	1928 ......33.5	1840 ......43.8	**1500** 503
1995 ......1.36	1961 ......15.6	1927 ......33.0	1830 ......49.1	1490 503
1994 ......1.40	**1960** 16.2	1926 ......32.5	1820 ......41.1	1480 503
1993 ......1.43	1959 ......16.4	1925 ......31.4	1810 ......33.5	1470 503
1992 ......1.45	1958 ......16.5	1924 ......32.0	**1800** 35.3	1460 503
1991 ......1.51	1957 ......16.9	1923 ......32.0	1790 ......62.9	1450 503
1990 ......1.59	1956 ......17.5	1922 ......30.5	1780 ......69.4	1440 503
1989 ....1.7	1955 ......18.5	1921 ......24.6	1770 ......69.4	1430 503
1988 ....1.9	1954 ......19.2	**1920** 22.4	1760 ......83.9	1420 503
1987 ....2.0	1953 ......19.5	1919 ......25.8	1750 ......95.9	1410 503
1986 ....2.1	1952 ......20.1	1918 ......25.8	1740 ......95.9	**1400** 503
1985 ....2.1	1951 ......22.1	1917 ......31.4	1730 ......95.9	1390 503
1984 ....2.3	**1950** 24.0	1916 ......38.0	1720 ......91.5	1380 503
1983 ....2.4	1949 ......24.9	1915 ......44.7	1710 ......83.9	1370 403
1982 ....2.5	1948 ......25.5	1914 ......55.9	**1700** 87.5	1360 403
1981 ....2.7	1947 ......38.9	1913 ......55.9	1690 ......95.9	1350 503
1980 ....3.0	1946 ......27.2	1912 ......55.9	1680 ......91.5	1340 671
1979 ....3.5	1945 ......27.6	1911 ......57.5	1670 ......91.5	1330 503
1978 ....4.0	1944 ......27.8	**1910** 59.2	1660 ......83.9	1320 403
1977 ....4.4	1943 ......28.0	1909 ......59.2	1650 ......83.9	1310 503
1976 ....5.1	1942 ......28.0	1908 ......59.2	1640 ......95.9	**1300** 503
1975 ....5.9	1941 ......28.0	1907 ......61.0	1630 101	1290 671
1974 ....7.3	**1940** 30.5	1906 ......67.1	1620 106	1280 503
1973 ....8.5	1939 ......35.3	1905 ......62.9	1610 106	1270 503

Animal speeds

Snail	Dad walking	Cyclist	Fastest sprinter	Dragonfly
0.03 mph	4 mph	10 mph	23 mph	36 mph

Machine speeds

This is a typical cyclist. The fastest ever was 132 mph, achieved by cycling down a glacier

First train . . . . 30 mph
Fastest steam train . . . . 126 mph (Mallard)
Fastest production car . . . . . 240 mph (McLaren F1)
Fastest boat . . . . 317.6 mph (Spirit of Australia, 1978)
Fastest train . . . . 321.8 mph (French TGV)
Jumbo jet . . . . 565 mph
Thrust SSC . . . . 763 mph (land speed record, 1997)
Concorde . . . . 1,336 mph
Fastest plane . . . . 2,193 mph (SR-71 Blackbird, 1976)
Space shuttle . . . . 18,000 mph
Fastest manmade object. . . . 153,800 mph (Helios 2 probe, 1976)

FASCINATING FACT

The fastest man in the world is not, as you might think, the 100-meter sprinter, but the 200-meter. The 100-meter man's average speed is cut by the time it takes him to get up to speed, a smaller factor over 200 meters.

Animal longevity, typical (years)

Tapeworm 2		Lobster, lion, rhino 15	
Mouse 3		Polar bear, gorilla, horse . 20	
Rabbit. 5		Grizzly bear 25	
Kangaroo, red fox. 7		Asian elephant. 40	
Squirrel, pig, giraffe. . . . 10		Killer whale, sturgeon . . . 50	
Cat, dog, camel. 12		Box turtle. 100	

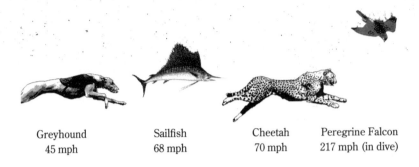

Greyhound	Sailfish	Cheetah	Peregrine Falcon
45 mph	68 mph	70 mph	217 mph (in dive)

Relative height

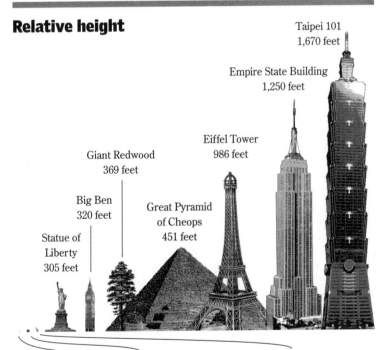

Taipei 101
1,670 feet

Empire State Building
1,250 feet

Eiffel Tower
986 feet

Giant Redwood
369 feet

Big Ben
320 feet

Great Pyramid
of Cheops
451 feet

Statue of
Liberty
305 feet

Average Dad: 6 feet; double-decker bus: 14 feet 4.5 inches; giraffe: 19 feet

How big is the Universe?

Very, very, very, very, very, very big.

If the Sun was shrunk to the size of a basketball, our own Solar System would still be a mile across and the nearest star 5,000 miles away.

According to astronomers, to get an idea of how many stars there are, you should try to imagine the total number of grains of sand on every beach in the world. Got it? Well, there are said to be a million stars for every one of those grains.

There are 400 billion stars in our own galaxy, the Milky Way, and the Hubble telescope has shown that there are 200 billion or more galaxies in the Universe. If the Milky Way is an average-sized galaxy, that means there must be some 80,000 billion, billion stars in the Universe.

We said it was big.

The Earth

The third planet from the Sun, the Earth is 4.5 billion years old, like the rest of our Solar System. This is reasonably young in comparison to the Universe, currently estimated to be almost 14 billion years old. The planet travels through space at 67,000 miles an hour as it orbits the Sun once a year.

The Earth rotates on its own axis every 23 hours 56 minutes and 4.1 seconds. It takes almost another four minutes until noon becomes noon again. This is because, in a day, the Earth has traveled 1.6 million miles in its annual 584 million mile elliptical orbit around the Sun, so each day it has to turn a bit further than 360° before the same spot faces the Sun.

The Earth's radius at the equator is 3,964 miles, and its circumference 24,901 miles. If you could walk right around the planet, doing 10 miles a day, it would take you almost seven years to arrive back where you started from.

Imagine a string of people standing on the equator holding hands. Assuming each person with outstretched arms took up 5 feet, you'd need 26 million people to complete the chain. With a population of 6.5 billion people, the chain could loop the Earth 250 times. As 200,000 more people are born than die every day, by 2050 the population will have grown so that the chain will loop round 350 times.

If you cut the Earth in half, it would look like a peculiar hard-boiled egg. The Earth's crust (the shell) is very thin and only 20 miles or so thick. The Earth's mantle (the white bit) is 1,800 miles thick. Inside that is the core (the yolk). There's no way we can journey to the center of the Earth. In fact, the deepest that geologists have drilled is under 8 miles, not even halfway to the mantle. The core is reckoned to be made mostly of iron. It is incredibly hot, over 7,000°F, the outer part of it being molten.

The Sun

The Sun is 93 million miles away. If we could drive a car to the Sun at 70 mph it would take 150 years to reach it. It's 860,000 miles across, 109 times the 7,900-mile diameter of the Earth. A million Earths could fit inside it.

The Sun is a ball of gas, three-quarters hydrogen and a quarter helium, with a core temperature of over 20 million°F, while the surface is almost 10,000°F.

Like all stars, the Sun is a massive nuclear reactor, turning 600 million tons of hydrogen into helium every second through nuclear fusion, releasing energy in the form of heat and light.

The Sun has used up half its lifetime's supply of hydrogen. In a mere 5 billion years or so, it will run out of fuel and become an unstable red giant, expanding outward and vaporizing all life on Earth. Don't say we didn't warn you.

Relative sizes of the Sun and the Earth (right). If the Sun were the size shown here, the Earth would be 58 pages away.

Moon facts and figures

It is 2,160 miles across compared to Earth's 7,900, and the Moon's distance from Earth varies between 222,000 and 252,000 miles. The average is about 238,000 miles, roughly 30 times the diameter of the Earth.

Full moons occur when the side of the Moon illuminated by the sun directly faces the Earth. The time between full moons is actually 29.53 days. During the 27.32 days the Moon takes to revolve around us, the Earth has moved in relation to the Sun. It's another two days and more before the Moon catches up to the same position relative to the Earth again. The time between new moons—when we can't see the Moon at all at night—is the same. This occurs when the Moon is between the Sun and the Earth, the Sun illuminating the side we can't see.

The Moon has no air, indeed no atmosphere at all, so there is no rain nor weather of any kind. Its temperature varies wildly, from 100°C (212°F, hot enough to boil water) to minus 147°C (–233°F).

Gravity is a sixth of that on Earth, from which the moon moves an inch and a half further away every year.

Relative sizes of the Earth (left) and the Moon (right). If the Earth were the size shown here, the Moon would be 15 pages away.

Relative weights

Averages are just that. You may weigh more or less than the average Dad, although it's unlikely you know your weight in tons.

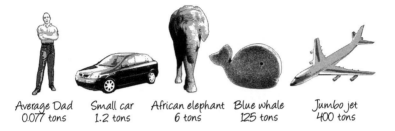

| Average Dad | Small car | African elephant | Blue whale | Jumbo jet |
| 0.077 tons | 1.2 tons | 6 tons | 125 tons | 400 tons |

Not included here is the world's largest vehicle—the Jahre Viking supertanker, which weighs in at an astonishing 555,000 tons.

Wacky number trivia

- You can write every number from 1 to 99 in words without using the letter "a."

- 111,111,111 x 111,111,111 = 12,345,678,987,654,321.

- Every time a fictional phone number is given in an American film or TV program, it includes 555.

- Celtic shepherds counted their sheep thus: Yan, tan, tethera, pethera, pimp, sethera, lethera, hovera, dovera, dic, yan-a-dic, tan-a-dic, tethera-dic. After every 13 sheep (the number chosen to confuse the gods) they'd make a mark on a stick and start again. A great way of counting children you're trying to herd!

- The 100 Years' War lasted 116 years. (The shortest war, when Zanzibar surrendered to Britain in 1896, lasted just 38 minutes.)

- "Forty" is the only number to have its letters in alphabetical order.

- There are 170,000,000,000,000,000,000,000,000 different ways of playing the first 10 moves in a game of chess.

- If all the Legos in the world were divided up evenly, we'd get 30 pieces each.

How to count up to 1,023 on your fingers

How high can you count on the fingers of both hands? Ten? Not very practical when you're totting up the number of white cars you pass on the freeway or the number of fries in the average McDonald's portion.

There is a better way. It turns out that a digital calculator is one of the accessories included with the human body.

Your fingers are, you may be surprised to know, numbered in powers of two, binary fashion. On your right hand, the thumb is 1, the index finger is 2, the next is 4, the next 8, and the last 16. On your left hand, from thumb outward, the numbers go 32, 64, 128, 256 and 512. If you have trouble remembering these numbers, get your kids to write them on your fingers.

Hold your hands, palm down, above a flat surface. Touch your thumb to the surface: that's 1. Raise your thumb and touch the index finger down: that's 2. Add

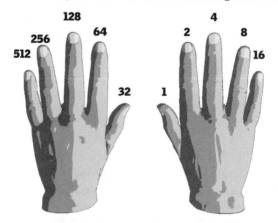

the thumb again, and that's 1 + 2 = 3. The chart opposite shows how to make the numbers from 1 to 31; when you add the left hand, you can get all the way up to 1,023 (it's one less than 1,024, which is 2 to the power of 10). It takes a bit of practice but soon becomes second nature. Indeed, practicing the finger sequence is a great way of nodding off at night. Don't actually count. Just do the movements.

When you've finished tapping out your fingers, add up the value of those fingers that are pressed down to get the grand total. Of course, if you're equally dextrous with your toes, you'd be able to count up to 1,048,575 . . .

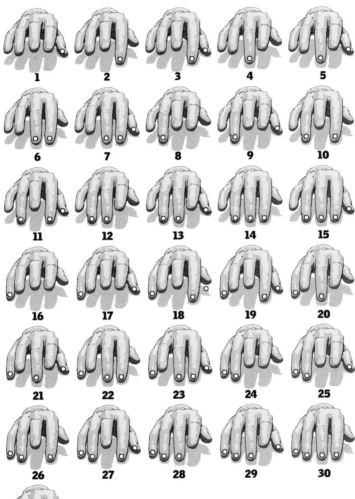

These are the movements for the right hand: mirror them for the left hand for the remaining numbers.

What is the biggest number of all?

It's hard to envisage even a million of something.* A million quarters, for instance, would form a stack just over a mile high. A million seconds is about 11.5 days. If you counted at the rate of one number a second with no breaks, it would take you 12 days to get to a million.

At the same rate, it would take 32 years to count to a billion. In Britain and some other places a billion used to be a million million, but these days pretty much everybody accepts a billion as 1,000 million (1 with 9 zeroes).

A trillion is a thousand billion, i.e. 1 with 12 zeros. You can continue on upward, if you're so inclined, with quadrillions, quintillions and so on—see page 112 for some more of this stuff. But it's all a bit unwieldy, so scientists and mathematicians prefer to work in powers.

In the 1940s, mathematician Edward Kasner asked his nine-year-old nephew what he should call 1 with 100 zeros. The boy said "Googol" and the name has stuck. It's a big number, greater even than the number of atoms in the entire Universe. It's so big it has lent its name, slightly adapted, to the most popular Internet search engine.

Even bigger still is the googolplex, 1 followed by a googol of zeroes, a number so mind-bogglingly enormous you can't even write it down in full. (One of the many throwaway gags in *The Simpsons* has the family going into a multi-screen cinema called the Googolplex. Just one more fact you can annoy your kids with while they're trying to watch the show.) A googolplex has more *digits* than there are atoms in the Universe. True, mathematicians have played around with larger numbers still, but they're just showing off.

It's hard to know where, in all this, a zillion comes. Bigger than a trillion, obviously, but not as big as a gazillion, which itself can surely be only a fraction of a squillion.

But let's try anyway. To help you visualize a million, the page opposite has 5,102 dots on it. If every page in this book were printed just like this one, the book would contain a million dots. But our publishers insisted on words as well.

Look at the page of dots for one minute. Can you see a face in it?

No? We couldn't either.

How long is a piece of string?

Don't be silly.

Number names

How many zeros in a billion? Why do we talk about *kilo*grams, but *milli*meters? Why aren't there 1000 bytes in a kilobyte? All can be revealed . . .

Name	Prefix	Symbol	Power	Number
septillion	yotta	Y	10^{24}	1 000 000 000 000 000 000 000 000
sextillion	zetta	Z	10^{21}	1 000 000 000 000 000 000 000
quintillion	exa	E	10^{18}	1 000 000 000 000 000 000
quadrillion	peta	P	10^{15}	1 000 000 000 000 000
trillion	tera	T	10^{12}	1 000 000 000 000
billion	giga	G	10^{9}	1 000 000 000
million	mega	M	10^{6}	1 000 000
thousand	kilo	k	10^{3}	1 000
hundred	hecto	h	10^{2}	100
ten	deca	da	10^{1}	10
one			10^{0}	1
tenth	deci	d	10^{-1}	0.1
hundredth	centi	c	10^{-2}	0.01
thousandth	milli	m	10^{-3}	0.001
millionth	micro	µ	10^{-6}	0.000 001
billionth	nano	n	10^{-9}	0.000 000 001
trillionth	pico	p	10^{-12}	0.000 000 000 001
this is	femto	f	10^{-15}	0.000 000 000 000 001
starting to	atto	a	10^{-18}	0.000 000 000 000 000 001
get really	zepto	z	10^{-21}	0.000 000 000 000 000 000 001
silly now	yocto	y	10^{-24}	0.000 000 000 000 000 000 000 001

Although computers use the same prefixes—kilo, mega, giga, tera—the numbers aren't exactly the same. This is because computers use 10th powers of 2, rather than powers of 10; and 2^{10} is 1024, not 1000.

In 1998 the International Electrotechnical Commission moved to rename these prefixes to kibi, mebi, gibi and tibi, for "kilobinary," "megabinary" and so on. Yeah, right. Like that's *really* going to make it less confusing.

kilobyte	2^{10}	1 024
megabyte	2^{20}	1 048 576
gigabyte	2^{30}	1 073 741 824
terabyte	2^{40}	1 099 511 627 776

Bits and bytes

Computer storage is measured in "Kb" (sometimes just written as "K")—short for kilobytes. Which, as we've shown opposite, is 1,024 bytes. So why is it that a 56K modem runs so slowly?

The answer is that the "56K" stands, confusingly, for 56 kilo*bits* per second, not 56 kilo*bytes*. A "bit" is a single piece of binary information: a 1 or a 0. There are eight bits in a byte, so a 56K modem, running at 56 kilobits per second, will therefore transmit data at just 8 kilo*bytes* per second.

Except the cheating doesn't stop there. For every 8 bits that a modem streams down the phone line, it automatically adds in two extra "framing" bits, one at the beginning and one at the end, so the receiving computer can tell where each byte starts and stops. In other words, for each byte of data, the modem has to send 10 bits in all. So in fact, a 56K modem actually delivers a paltry 5.6 kilobytes per second. Time to upgrade to broadband!

Roman numerals

Before the Western world adopted the Arabic system of numbering we use today, the Romans used systems of letters to stand for numbers. They are:

I = 1   V = 5   X = 10   L = 50   C = 100   D = 500   M = 1000

It's difficult enough when writing dates—the year 1897, for instance, would be written MDCCCXCVII—but almost impossible for doing math. Try multiplying LXXV by VIII in your head and see how long it takes you, compared with the simple 75 x 8.

If you add the first six Roman numerals together—DCLXVI—you get 666, a figure referred to in the Bible as the Number of the Beast. Spooky? Or just coincidence?

The figure 4 is always written as IV, except on clock faces, where it's almost always written as IIII. This is a hangover from medieval Latin: the earliest surviving clock face is in Wells Cathedral in England, dating from before 1392, and shows four o'clock in this fashion.

One of the very few exceptions is the clock face on London's Palace of Westminster, better known as Big Ben, which shows the figure four as IV.

World facts and figures

Biggest wave: A wave 1,720 ft. high swept over Lituya Bay, Alaska, in 1958

Richest: The USA has 341 billionaires, not all of whom work for Microsoft

Highest waterfall: Water at Angel Falls, Venezuela, drops 3,281 feet

Wettest: Mt. Waialeale in Hawaii has an annual rainfall of 472 inches

Highest (1): Mt. Mauna Loa, in Hawaii, rises 2.5 miles above sea level—but there's another 3.7 miles of it underwater

Driest: The Pacific coast of Chile, between Antofagasta and Arica, records just 0.004 inches of rain a year. It hasn't rained in the Atacama Desert for 400 years

Greatest river: The Amazon pours 4.2 million cubic feet *per second* into the Atlantic Ocean

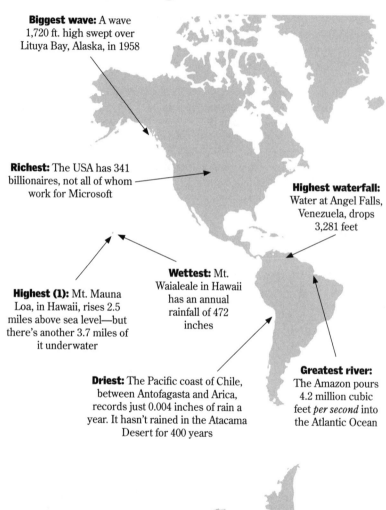

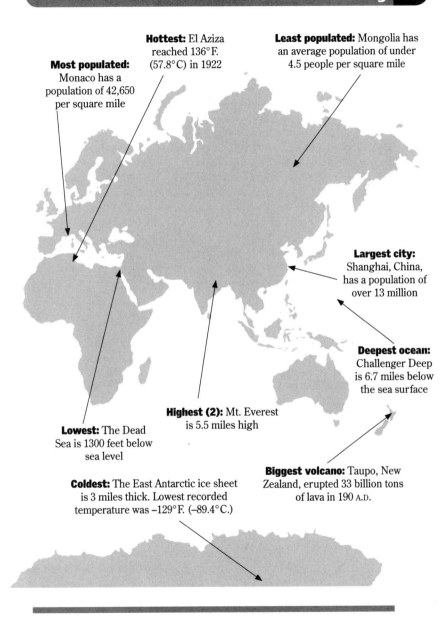

Hottest: El Aziza reached 136°F. (57.8°C) in 1922

Least populated: Mongolia has an average population of under 4.5 people per square mile

Most populated: Monaco has a population of 42,650 per square mile

Largest city: Shanghai, China, has a population of over 13 million

Deepest ocean: Challenger Deep is 6.7 miles below the sea surface

Highest (2): Mt. Everest is 5.5 miles high

Lowest: The Dead Sea is 1300 feet below sea level

Coldest: The East Antarctic ice sheet is 3 miles thick. Lowest recorded temperature was –129°F. (–89.4°C.)

Biggest volcano: Taupo, New Zealand, erupted 33 billion tons of lava in 190 A.D.

The speed of light

Light zips along at 186,000 miles a second. That's 700 million miles an hour, getting on for a million times faster than the speed of sound. In the time it takes a ball dropped from 6 feet to reach the ground, light could bounce all the way around the Earth five times.

Unless it's directed through a fiber-optic cable, however, light travels in straight lines. Its speed may seem instant, but it isn't. It takes light 1.28 seconds to reach us from the Moon and eight minutes from the Sun, 93 million miles away.

Our nearest star other than the Sun, Proxima Centauri, is 25 trillion miles away. As light travels 5.9 trillion miles in a year, it takes 4.2 years for its light to reach us (that is, 4.2 light years). When we look at the stars, we are looking at the past. It is 30,000 light years from the center of our own galaxy, for instance, while the nearest galaxy to ours, Andromeda, is 2.2 million light years away.

The most distant objects astronomers have been able to see are about 13 billion light years away. That means that the light we see now left there 13 billion years ago, just 700 million years after the Universe was born.

How to calculate the speed of light

Yes, it can be done, with no more exotic equipment than a microwave and a plate of grated cheese. For microwaves, like radio waves, move at the speed of light.

Take the turntable out of the microwave, spread the cheese evenly on the plate, and cook for around 20 seconds (until the cheese starts to melt). You'll see some

hot spots of melted cheese among the raw stuff: measure the distance between these in centimeters. You'll find a predominant distance, probably between 6 and 12 cm, depending on your model. This corresponds to half the wavelength of the microwave. If you multiply the full wavelength by the number of times it travels that distance in a second, known as the frequency, you get the speed of light.

But how do you know the frequency? Fortunately, microwave

manufacturers provide this information for you. Turn the microwave around and look at the back. You'll find a label specifying the frequency of the microwave: it's generally around 2450 MHz.

All you have to do now is multiply the distance (in meters, so divide your centimeters by 100) by the wavelength, and that's the speed of light.

Our microwave produced an average distance of 6 cm, which means a wavelength of 12 cm (0.12 meters). Multiplying that by 2450 MHz gives a figure of 294. The "M" in MHz stands for a million (see page 112): so the speed of light comes out at 294,000,000 meters per second.

In fact, the real speed of light is 299,800,000 meters per second, so our calculations are pretty close!

Are we there yet?

How fast can rockets travel?

Although light travels at 700 million miles an hour, our chemically powered spaceships are somewhat slower. NASA's space shuttle orbits the earth at a mere 18,000 miles an hour. The *Voyager* space probe, launched in 1977, was the first man-made spacecraft to leave the Solar System and is still out there, traveling at 38,000 miles an hour. At that speed it would take 76,000 years to reach the nearest star, Proxima Centauri, and 500 million years to reach the center of our own Galaxy.

Scientists tell us that no matter how fast spaceships go, they will never be able to travel faster than light. "Warp speed" and interstellar travel are therefore likely, for some time to come at least, to be nothing more than science fiction.

But science fiction often becomes science fact, like the solar-powered ion engine which propelled the experimental probe *Deep Space One*. Sending out a stream of high-speed particles, it could accelerate at only 15 mph per day, the thrust of its engine being no more powerful than a piece of paper would feel resting in your hand. But that thrust—10 times as efficient as conventional rockets—was constant and eventually got *Deep Space One* up to a speed of 35,000 miles an hour. All that from a propulsion system not unlike the exchange of electrons that gives you a shock when you touch metal after walking on a thick carpet (see page 10).

Human facts: hair . . .

There are thought to be over 100,000 hairs on the average human head, growing at the rate of 6 inches a year.

A German scientist once went to the trouble of counting the hairs on women's heads (at least, that was his excuse at the time). He discovered that blonde women have more hairs (140,000 strands) than brown (110,000), black (108,000) or redheads (90,000).

Sadly, many Dads will find the number of hairs on their own heads declining as the years advance. Whether hair loss is directly related to parenthood has yet to be scientifically proven.

. . . bones . . .

You start off with over 300 bones, but they fuse together as you grow. As an adult, you have 206 bones in your body, more than half of them in your hands and feet. Oddly, humans and giraffes have the same number of bones in their necks. The giraffe's are just that bit longer.

. . . sneezes . . .

A sneeze travels at around 100 mph, faster than a hurricane. It's also impossible to sneeze with your eyes open.

. . . blood . . .

Your heart beats around 40 million times a year. If you live 70 years, that will mean almost 3 billion beats. Every day, it pumps the equivalent of 2,000 gallons of blood around your body.

If all the blood vessels in the body were joined end to end, they would stretch 100,000 miles for an adult (60,000 for a child). That's enough to go around the Earth four times.

. . . and guts

If it were removed from the body, the small intestine would stretch to a length of 22 feet.

9 Puzzles, tricks, and jokes

GIVING YOUR CHILDREN PUZZLES is a great way to help expand their minds and hone their skills in logic and deduction. We've included both quickfire questions and mind-numbingly tricky teasers, which are guaranteed to test their brainpower and their tenacity.

Fun though it is to watch kids' brains working, they need to be entertained as well as educated. So here's a selection of riddles and jokes that will make them laugh, groan or—in some cases—merely gaze at you in bafflement. But don't be surprised if you hear an outbreak of giggling from their bedroom later that night, when they finally get the point of one of your more obscure gags.

Magic always fascinates children. They want to believe in it. And you want them to believe, because magic keeps your mortal status hidden for a few more years. So we've got tricks ranging from the truly astounding to the downright dumb. We've also included a couple of great mind-reading routines in which they, not you, can be the stars of the show.

Urban legends

Once bedtime fairy stories become a little passé, move on to urban legends. Most kids love these frequently spooky tales, particularly as they aren't about some woodcutter's daughter who lived once upon a time in a far-off land. They're usually about real places, real people and real lives; and while some say urban legends aren't real, we say there aren't that many houses made of gingerbread.

The key to urban myth telling is embellishment: the more you can do to make them relevant to your children's experience, the better. Rather than repeat these shaggy dog stories in full, we're listing the key moments to keep you on track. How local and scary you make them is up to you.

The choking Doberman

- A dark, stormy night (it usually is).
- Woman alone. Thinks she hears a noise.
- It's her Doberman (could be your own breed, but usually a Doberman). It's having trouble breathing.
- She rushes him to the vet. He tells her there will have to be an emergency operation. She should go home and wait for his call.
- Home, she gets ready for bed. She feels unnerved without the dog there.
- Phone rings. It's the vet, telling her to get out of the house immediately.
- As she emerges, the police arrive, sirens blazing.
- They rush inside and drag out a burglar hiding under the bed, who's clutching his bloody hand. The vet found the obstruction in the dog's throat: it was two bloody, severed fingers.

The breakdown in the woods

- A dark night, possibly even a little stormy.
- A couple driving through woods. On the radio, they hear of an escaped murderer.
- The car breaks down in a remote location. (Nobody had mobile phones when the story first appeared—they'd find that difficult to believe!—so you'll have to explain that it's an area with no reception.)
- The boyfriend says he'll go for help, telling her to lock the doors.
- He's gone a very long time, and she gets frightened. Then she hears a tapping

noise on the roof of the car. Whenever the wind blows, there it is again . . . tap, tap, tap.

● She is terrified. Daren't get out to look. Finally falls asleep. Woken in morning by a policeman knocking on her window. Tells her to get out of the car and, whatever she does, she mustn't look back.

● As she's getting into the police car, she can't help herself, and turns. Hanging from the tree is her boyfriend, dead, his dangling feet knocking on the roof of the car . . . tap, tap, tap.

The dead diver

● Massive forest fire, despite the darkness and storminess of the night.

● Police puzzled to find a corpse dressed in scuba gear—tanks, wet suit, flippers, face mask—the lot.

● Post-mortem reveals that he didn't die from heat or flames, but from massive internal injuries.

● Corpse identified from dental records. Been reported missing while out diving off the coast six miles away (distance doesn't matter, but sounds more realistic if you give precise figures).

● Discovered that a fire-fighting helicopter scooping up water had inadvertently picked him up too. The chopper pilot didn't hear his screams and dumped him on the flames.

The mangled rabbit

● Man goes into his garden and finds his dog with a piece of mangled fur in its mouth. It's stormy, and also dark, so he has difficulty identifying it.

● Turns out to be a dead rabbit from next door.

● Man is horrified, thinks his dog has killed it.

● Spends an hour washing and drying the rabbit to make it look like it died of natural causes.

● Places rabbit back in neighbor's cage and sneaks back indoors.

● Neighbor comes home from work, finds rabbit in cage. General commotion, grief-stricken wailing, etc.

● Man looks over fence, commiserates with neighbor over the death of the pet.

● "I can't understand it," explains the neighbor. "The rabbit died last night, and I buried it this morning."

Puzzle 1: The three children

This simple puzzle still catches most kids out the first time because, even though you entreat them to listen carefully, they don't:

John's mother has three children. The eldest is called April, the middle child is called May. What's the youngest called?

Nearly all kids—and a surprising number of adults—barely pause before replying "June." The correct answer, of course, is John.

Puzzle 2: Which switch?

How many Dads does it take to change me?

Some puzzles can be solved immediately; others necessitate rather more brain wracking. This deliciously fiendish, but hugely satisfying, puzzle falls into the latter category. Most children, and adults, will need a helping hand to get the answer.

Inside a room is a lightbulb. Outside are three switches in the off position. There is no way to see into the room without opening the door. How do you work out which switch turns on the light? You can fiddle with the switches as much as you like, but you're only allowed to open the door to the room once.

You will invariably have to fend off all manner of intriguing and ridiculous suggestions. No, you can't slide mirrors under the door. Nor can you pack ice around the bulb or install video cameras in the room.

Explain that everything needed for the solution is in the question and encourage them to think about the physics of lightbulbs. When you turn on a bulb, apart from it lighting up, what else happens? When they figure out that the bulb also gets hot, they're nearly there.

The solution is now straightforward. Turn on the first switch, wait a minute, then turn it off. Turn on the second switch and enter the room. If the bulb is on, the second switch is the one that did the job; if the bulb is off but warm, it's the first switch; if the bulb is off but cold, it must be the third switch that operates it.

Puzzle 3: The camel race

It always helps to listen to the precise wording of the question. This is particularly true in this puzzle.

Two princes are desperate to marry the Sultan's daughter. The Sultan invites them to attend him in a tent in the desert. He explains that the contest will be decided by a race: whichever prince's camel reaches the palace last shall marry his daughter. After just a moment's thought, the princes rush out and race to the palace, certain that the first to get there will win the Sultan's daughter's hand. What was their solution?

One hump or two?

The first approach is usually to suggest that the princes ride as slowly as possible. But this is clearly no solution at all. The answer, of course, lies in the Sultan's exact phrasing: the winner is the prince whose camel is last.

The simple, kick-yourself-afterward solution is that the princes jump onto each other's camels. If they win the race, their *camel* will not.

Puzzle 4: The hardware store

This is one of those really neat, compact puzzles that will have even mathematical geniuses scratching their heads in anguish, before—or if—they make that leap of imagination and get the answer right.

A man goes into a hardware store to buy some items for his house.
"How much is one?" he asks, and is told "$3."
"How much for twelve?"
"$6," says the assistant.
"And how much for two hundred?"
"$9," comes the reply.
There are no bulk discounts involved. What is he buying?

It's one of those duh! answers. He's buying house numbers.

Puzzle 5: Pick up the olive

. . . or the peanut, or cherry tomato, or even a Ping-Pong ball. Any object that's more or less spherical, and small enough to fit inside a brandy glass, will do for this puzzle.

Place the olive on the table, and stand a brandy glass next to it. The glass has to be of the bowl variety, with an opening that's much narrower than the middle. The task is to get the olive into the glass without blowing it, tilting the table, or allowing it to be touched by any object other than the glass.

The solution, when everyone's given up, is splendid. Turn the wine glass upside down over the olive, and move it rapidly in small circles, spinning the olive with it. The olive will run around the edge of the glass and, due to centrifugal force, rise up to the widest part; still spinning, you can now lift the glass off the table, with the olive still going around inside it, and turn it the right way up. Brilliant!

Puzzle 6: The logical explorers

Four logical explorers are captured by, as luck would have it, a tribe of logical cannibals. The cannibals tell them that they'll eat the explorers unless they solve a puzzle. And this is the puzzle.

The explorers are buried up to their necks in sand, three facing one way and one facing the other. There's a brick wall between explorer A and the other three.

You can't eat me,
I'm a vegetarian

A   B   C   D

The cannibals explain that four hats, two red and two blue, will be placed on the explorers at random. Each day the hats will be swapped around, and unless one of the explorers can tell the cannibals what color hat he's wearing, that night's menu will feature explorer casserole.

The explorers can't see their own hats, nor can they turn their heads. They're not allowed to communicate with each other, and only one word can be spoken by the whole group. And yet, remarkably, each day one of them manages to shout out the color of his hat. How?

Let's say explorers B and C both have blue hats. Then explorer D, knowing there are only two blue hats, knows his must be red—and shouts out that color accordingly. But what if explorers B and C have different-colored hats? Explorer D can't then know the color of his own hat.

And that's the clever part. Explorer C waits to hear what explorer D does. If he says nothing, then explorer C knows that he and explorer B must have different-colored hats. He can see the color of explorer B's hat, and so shouts out the opposite color. Explorers A and B, in the meantime, say and do nothing. But beneath the sand you can be sure they're crossing their fingers.

Puzzle 7: Walking the dog

Some puzzles appear to be more complex than they really are. Often, it's simply a matter of thinking around the problem.

A man takes his dog for a walk in the park. He walks around a circular pond, which takes him exactly an hour. (It's a very big pond.) He has a stick which he throws for the dog, and which the dog retrieves and brings back to him without breaking its run (it's a very well-trained dog). The dog runs at 10 miles an hour. If the man wants the dog to get the maximum amount of exercise, should he throw the stick in front of him, behind him, or across the other side of the pond?

They'll hate the answer: it doesn't make any difference.

The dog keeps running for as long as the man keeps walking. The man walks for an hour, in which time the dog runs 10 miles—no matter in which direction the man throws the stick.

Quick-fire puzzles

Some of these simply require thinking through; with others, you'll need to allow your children to ask questions so you can guide them toward the correct solution. Feel free to give as many clues as you like!

● *A man stopped his car opposite a hotel and immediately knew that he was bankrupt. How?*
He was playing Monopoly.

● *Dad has 20 socks in his drawer, 10 black and 10 gray. If he dresses in the dark, how many does he have to take out to ensure that he has a pair?*
Three.

● *Which triangle is bigger, one that has sides of 2, 3 and 4 inches or one with sides of 3, 4 and 7 inches?*
The first. The second is a straight line.

● *Before Mount Everest was discovered, what was the highest mountain on Earth?*
Mount Everest.

● *A mountaineer climbed a mountain with a guide. But traversing a deep crevasse, the guide fell and disappeared from sight. Undaunted, the mountaineer carried on, and gave no thought to getting help. Why?*
The guide was a book.

● *A man buys several loaves of bread at $1 a loaf, and sells them at 25¢ a loaf. He does it again and again.*

Entirely as a result of this, he becomes a millionaire. How?
He started off as a billionaire, who decided to help the poor.

● *What five-letter word becomes shorter when you add two letters?*
Short.

● *Removing tonsils is a tonsillectomy. Removing an appendix is an appendectomy. What do you call it when a growth is removed from your head?*
A haircut.

● *You're in a race. Almost at the tape, you overtake the person who's second. What position do you finish?*
Second.

● *If two's company and three's a crowd, then what's four and five?*
Nine.

● *A man travels to work in London. His train to work travels at 100 miles an hour and the journey takes one hour 20 minutes. In the other direction, going at the same speed, the trip takes 80 minutes. Why?*
One hour 20 minutes and 80 minutes are the same amount of time.

- *If post is spelled POST and most is spelled MOST, how do you spell the word for what you put in a toaster?*
Bread.

- *What invention lets you see through walls?*
A window.

- *How much earth in cubic feet is there in a hole 1 foot by 1 foot by 1 foot?*
None. It's a hole.

- *A farmer has four fields. In one, there are 8 haystacks, in the next 7, in the third 9 and in the last he has 11. If he puts them all together, how many haystacks will he have?*
One. But it's a big one.

- *A greengrocer is 6 feet tall, has a 40-inch chest and wears size 13 shoes. What do you think he weighs?*
Fruit and vegetables.

- *It's cold and you're hungry. You have only one match. In a room in your cabin is an oil lamp, a wood-burning stove and a candle. What do you light first?*
The match.

- *Which is greater, six dozen dozen or half a dozen dozen?*
Six dozen dozen is 12 times greater.

- *Which two numbers multiplied together give you 17?*
One and 17.

- *A yacht is moored in the harbor. Over its side hangs a rope ladder, with its end just touching the water. Rungs of the ladder are one foot apart. If the tide rises at the rate of one foot an hour, how many of the rungs will be covered after six hours?*
None. The ladder's fixed to the boat and rises with the tide.

- *There are five apples in a basket and five people in the room. How can you give an apple to each one and have one apple remain in the basket?*
You give the basket with one apple in it to the last person.

- *If three cats can kill three rats in three minutes, how long will it take 100 cats to kill 100 rats?*
Three minutes.

- *A bus got lost and tried to drive under a low bridge. Unfortunately, it got stuck and couldn't move forward or backward. It was a schoolgirl on the bus who told the bus driver how they could free the vehicle. What was her solution?*
Letting some air out of the tires to lower the bus slightly.

- *What do you call a deer with no eyes?*
No idea.

- *What do you call a deer with no eyes that's not moving?*
Still no idea.

Knock knock

Children adore knock-knock jokes but, unless you can retaliate with a few well-chosen ones of your own, you may find yourself becoming reluctant to open the door. Here are just a handful of what we suspect are tens of thousands of knock-knock jokes, most of which your children will at some point try to tell you.

Danielle. *Danielle who?* (No answer). *DANIELLE WHO?* Danielle so loud, I heard you the first time.

Wendy. *Wendy who?* When de wind blows, de cradle will rock.

Lemon juice. *Lemon juice who?* Lemon introduce myself.

Mikey. *Mikey who?* Mikey has broken off in the lock.

Sam and Janet. *Sam and Janet who?* Sam and Janet evening, you may see a stranger . . .

Jess. *Jess who?* Jess checking you're in.

Stopwatch. *Stopwatch who?* Stop watcha doing and let me in.

Irish stew. *Irish stew who?* Irish stew in the name of the law.

Matthew. *Matthew who?* Matthew laces are undone.

Sarah. *Sarah who?* Sarah doctor in the house?

Ash. *Ash who?* Bless you.

Spell. *Spell who?* Okay, w . . . h . . . o.

Wurlitzer. *Wurlitzer who?* Wurlitzer one for the money, two for the show...

Scott. *Scott who?* Scotta be some better jokes than this.

Dee. *Dee who?* Dee-sappear and stop telling me knock-knock jokes.

Dad. *Dad who?* Da doo ron ron ron, da doo ron ron. What d'you mean you don't understand it? It's a famous song, from the 60s. I'll sing you a bit of it . . . where's everybody gone?

When you've had enough knock-knock jokes to last you a lifetime and have to put an end to them or risk losing your sanity, there's an easy way to kill them off. If anyone says "Knock knock," simply answer, "Come in."

The personal knock-knock joke

Instead of opening the door to a vast number of people you don't know—and frankly don't wish to know—why not personalize the knock-knock joke, tailoring it to your child's own name?

Using our own children as an example, Freddy's very own knock-knock joke would be, "*Freddy who?*," "'Fraid he can't come, so he sent me instead." Joe equals "D'you . . . ," Izzy translates as "Is he . . . ," Joseph becomes "Just have . . . ," and Connie's joke uses "Can he . . ."

Any suggestion that we chose those names for our children because they were particularly suited to being used in knock-knock jokes is, of course, wholly without foundation.

The wrong answer

Almost everyone (child and adult) gets this seemingly simple math problem, which must be done in the head, wrong.

Start with 1,000, and add 40. Now add another 1,000. Now add 30. Then another 1,000. Now add 20. Then another 1,000. Lastly, add 10.

What is the total? Most people end up with 5,000 but the answer is actually 4,100. Without a calculator or pen and paper, people tend to round it up wrongly.

The lateral-thinking dentist

A woman had just moved to a new town and needed a dentist. There were only two dentists to choose from. One had a beautiful new office, he was a charming man, and his teeth were white and regular. The other office was desperately in need of paint, the dentist was grumpy, to a large extent because his crooked teeth hurt him. She chose to go to the second dentist. Why?

It's one of those puzzles that looks like there has to be a trick, but really there isn't. It may take some guidance to help your child work out that each dentist treats the other one's teeth—so it's the one with bad teeth who's the better dentist.

Puzzling pachyderms

Tell your child to pick a number from 1 to 10. Multiply it by 9 and then subtract 5. Add all the digits, to get a one-digit number. If it's not, do it again.

With numbers corresponding to letters of the alphabet (i.e., A = 1, B = 2), tell them to find the right letter of the alphabet for their number and to think of a country that begins with that letter. Then think of an animal that begins with the *second* letter of that country. Then think of a color associated with that animal.

Look at your child quizzically, and say: "But there *are* no gray elephants in Denmark." This is almost always the combination people end up with (unless they've played before and are deliberately trying to trip you up) and the sense of wonder is priceless.

The black hole

Black holes can swallow things up—in this instance, a pencil. When you do this trick, your child's mouth should open wide with astonishment.

With one or two kids seated to your left (or your right if you're left-handed), get out a sheet of paper and draw several concentric circles, perhaps a few arrows, all leading to the magic black hole in the middle. Explain that anything touching a black hole will be swallowed up. Warn them that, no matter what they do, they mustn't touch it. They should even take care if they stare at it.

Prepare your arm movement . . .   *. . . take a practice swing . . .*

Without taking your own eyes off it, silently roll up your shirt sleeves, pick up the pencil and study the black hole intently. Perhaps alter a mark or two on the paper. Build up the anticipation of what you're about to do.

Lean over the black hole and, with your finger and thumb, hold the pencil just above it, point upward. As you go through the count, your hand should go up and down as if you're readying a darts throw. In fact, you're actually preparing to lodge the pencil in that handy nook at the top of your ear (sorry, it isn't a real black hole).

Say "*One*," then bring the pencil up and onto the top of your ear. You are range-finding the spot. On "*Two*," bring it down to hover over the black hole, then back up, slide into a secure position. You can take your time here; attention is most focused on the counts, not what's happening in between. It will only increase the tension. On "*Three*," bring your (empty) hand down fast to the same position above the circle.

Freeze for a moment or two then, slowly, examine your own hand—and the other one—as if you're trying to figure out what's happened. You might even turn the paper over and examine where the hole in the table ought to be.

Hunt for the pencil with the kids. Look under the table so you're out of sight, and retrieve the pencil from its hiding place, perhaps even producing it out from the underside of the black hole. If there are others in the room, chances are that —only half paying attention—they will have caught the count and the pencil's disappearance, reinforcing the "magic" of what you've done.

. . . tuck the pencil behind your ear . . .   . . . and slam down on the table.

Mind reading for beginners

Despite being incredibly simple to carry off, this really is an impressive mind-reading trick. It can easily be performed by you and a child although, once they've got the hang of it, you risk being dropped from the act if your pupil decides they'd prefer to perform with another stooge. It's a tough game, showbiz.

The mind reader is either blindfolded, or else turns so that they can't see their partner. In full view of the audience, the assistant (Dad) holds up a number of fingers from one to ten and asks the mind reader to say how many. Time and again, the mind reader will announce the correct number.

The key to the trick is the way the question is put to the mind reader: it should have the same number of *words* as there are fingers being held up. If there are seven fingers, then the question should be, "How many fingers am I holding up?" If there are three, you can ask "How many now?"

Clearly, the routine will only work once a child is familiar with the difference between syllables and words. Ensure that the mind reader has their hands concealed. If they repeat the question while ticking off the words on their fingers, you're going to astound nobody but an elderly relative who is particularly slow on the uptake.

As with all such tricks, leave your audience wanting more. Doing it more than four or five times (fewer with adults) will greatly increase the risk of them guessing the secret.

Advanced mind reading

With the mind reader out of the room, the audience collectively decides upon an object. Returning, the mind reader concentrates as his assistant (Dad) calls out various objects, seemingly at random. After saying "no" to all the red herrings, the mind reader will quite confidently say "yes" when the assistant names the object agreed upon.

After doing this a couple of times, some of the audience will be convinced they know how it's done. The act gets more impressive still as you adapt it to take account of their suggestions. If they think the assistant is giving hand signals to the magician, have the assistant keep their hands behind their back. If they think it's somehow related to the object being chosen, let them pick somebody's shoes. The mind reader will still choose the right pair.

How is it done? Alarmingly simple. The magician merely says "yes" to the first thing named *after a black object*. Yup, that's all it is. But don't tell. With luck, you can keep this mind-reading act going for years, a bond of complicity between you and your child against the rest of the world.

The coin's fantastic voyage

Get a coin to travel from one foot to the other—inside your body.

Before anybody's looking, slip a coin under your left foot. If you decide to do the trick with bare feet, then removing your shoes and socks could be a good cover for this. Take a similar coin, visibly place it under your right foot and explain that you will make it work its way up your right leg and down the other one.

As you simulate this happening, twitch and twist as if something is passing through your body, going up one leg and down the other. When you've given the impression that it has reached your left foot, have it travel all the way back again until, pretending you expect wild applause, you lift your right foot and show that it has arrived back where it started.

The children will no doubt protest that this is no trick at all. The coin hasn't moved. With mock indignation, you start again, showing it traveling up your right leg and down your left. Pause for effect, then lift your left foot to show that the coin really has arrived there.

The only thing left to make your triumph complete is to ensure that you spirit away the coin that's still under your right foot. A piece of Silly Putty attached to the coin at the last moment will achieve this perfectly.

What do you call a fish with no eye?

All kids love telling jokes. If they're particularly keen, being on the receiving end is like attending a stand-up comedy venue on a wide-open mike night. You must be able to retaliate. But if the only joke you can recall is the one you heard in the pub about the priest, the hooker and the pineapple, the chances are that it will prove unsuitable.

Here's a selection, sometimes truncated for brevity, that will help you retaliate while still keeping your PG rating. We know some are old chestnuts. Heck, some of these jokes were old when *we* were children. But old to us is very often new to our kids.

- What do you call a man who can't stand? Neil. (Be warned that this could spark off a series of "What do you call . . . ?" jokes.)

- What's gray and has a trunk? A mouse going on vacation.

- What's brown and has a trunk? A mouse coming back from vacation.

- What's large, gray and doesn't matter? An irrelephant.

- What was Beethoven doing when they opened his coffin? Decomposing.

- A man rushes into a doctor's office.
  "Doctor, you've got to help me. I think I'm turning into a moth."
  "You need a psychiatrist. Why did you come to me?"
  "I couldn't help myself. Your light was on."

- What's green and sings? Elvis Parsley.

- What is orange and sounds like a parrot? A carrot.

- What's red and stupid? A blood clot.

- What's red and smells of paint? Red paint.

- What do you call a boomerang that won't come back? A stick.

- Two fish in a tank. One turns to the other and says,
  "Do you know how to drive this thing?"

- Why do ducks have webbed feet? To stamp out fires.

- Why do elephants have flat feet? To stamp out burning ducks.

- A woodworm goes into a pub, and says "Is the bartender here?" (You'll get this one eventually.)

- A Frenchman goes into a bar with a duck on his head. The barman says, "Wowee! Where did you get that?" The duck says, "Paris—they've got millions of them."

- A doctor tells his patient, "I've got some good news and some bad news."
  "What's the good news?"
  "You've only got 24 hours to live."
  "That's the *good news?* That's terrible! What's the bad news?"
  "I should have told you yesterday."

- What do Mack the Knife, Winnie the Pooh and Attila the Hun have in common? The same middle name.

- I've got a step ladder. It's nice, but I'm sad I don't know my real ladder.

- Man goes to the doctor with a strawberry growing out of the top of his head. Doctor says, "Let me give you some cream for that."

- What do you call a fish with no eye?
  "Fsh."

I see no chips

- Roses are red,
  Violets are green;
  Not only am I color blind,
  I'm a really bad poet as well.

- A little girl walks into a pet shop and asks in a sweet lisp, "Excuthe me, mithter. Do you keep wittle wabbits?" The shopkeeper smiles at her, and asks, "Do you want a wittle white wabby or a soft, fuwwy black wabby or maybe that cute wittle brown wabby over there?" She examines the rabbits, then says to him, "To be honest, I don't fink my pyfon's all that picky."

- Why did Robin Hood steal from the rich? Because the poor didn't have any money.

- Why can't you starve in a desert? Because of all the sand which is there.

- What nationality is Santa Claus? North Polish.

- What do you call a snowman with a sun tan? A puddle.

Math and magic

This math-based trick requires a little preparation, but it's a real humdinger. The way the trick works, of course, is that any three-figure number can be juggled to create just one answer, 1089. Before you begin, write down the ninth number on page 108 of the telephone directory and seal it in an envelope which you can give to an audience member or secrete somewhere.

Start off with some guff about your supernatural powers, and then ask for a three-digit number with all the digits different. Get one of your audience to write this down both forward and backward. You need to subtract the smaller from the larger. Although you can do it yourself, if the kids are old enough, it's better to get them to do it.

You will now have a number with 2 or 3 digits, with a 9 in the tens column. This should be written down backward. If it only has two digits, add a zero at the end. Add this to the result of the first calculation and you will get 1089. If not, somebody's math needs a little work!

Here's an example: if your audience chooses 237, then reverse that to get 732. Subtracting the smaller from the larger results in 495. Reversing this gives you 594; add these two together to get 1089.

Let a member of your audience go to the phone book, find page 108 and read out the ninth number, making sure they get the right number. When the envelope

is opened, they should be gobsmacked that the same number is inside, unless they're already holding down a top job in the city.

The book doesn't have to be a telephone directory. You could use a dictionary and work it so that it's the ninth word to be defined on page 108. Or you could take a risk and let your audience choose which book to use among the directories, encyclopedias and dictionaries in the room. Simply put a piece of paper with the answer in each book somewhere toward the back so it can be found by flicking through the pages.

If you're visiting somebody else's house in the same area, the telephone directory will be the same as yours. This means you can bring the number with you. Even more miraculous!

Pop-up popcorn

Here's one to try on the kids in the cinema. It works particularly well during scary scenes. As they'll no doubt expect you to go off and get the drinks and popcorn, you'll have plenty of time to tear a hole in the bottom of the popcorn carton.

Once some of the popcorn has been devoured and the children are absorbed in a particularly tense moment, work your hand up through the hole. When the next mitt delves in for popcorn, grab it. No doubt they'll scream their heads off but you can bet that the next time they go to the movies with their mates, they'll be trying it for themselves.

A vegetable kids do love

Answer these questions as quickly as possible.

What's 3 + 7?
What's 4 + 6?
What's 8 + 2?
Name a vegetable.

Did you answer "carrot"? Almost everyone does. If you write it down first, your kids will be even more impressed that you could read their minds.

The glass of water trick

Place a glass of water on the table, and lay a hat down over it. Tell your child you can drink the water without touching the hat. Then crawl beneath the table and make slurping sounds. Come back up, wiping your mouth as if you've drunk the water.

When your child lifts the hat to check whether you really have achieved the impossible, pick up the glass of water and drink it. There you go —you've drunk all the water without touching the hat. And in the process, you've probably ensured your child will grow up always making certain they read the small print.

String escapology

Cut lengths of string into pairs four or five feet long. Sort the challengers into twos. One should have the ends of a piece of string tied to both wrists. The other should tie a piece to one wrist, then pass the string over their partner's string before tying the other end to their free wrist so that they are roped together. Then tie yourself to your partner in the same way, ensuring there is just enough slack in the loops on their wrists to pass string through.

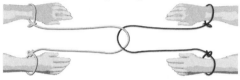

Tell the others that all they have to do is unlink their string from their partner's. They will go through some wonderfully entertaining contortions, turning back to back, stepping through the string, writhing this way and that.

When they've finally had enough and realize it isn't so simple after all, show them how it's done. Take the center of your string, and pass it through the loop on your partner's wrist and over their hand. With one bound, you'll be free.

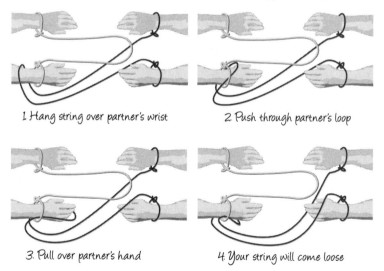

1. Hang string over partner's wrist

2. Push through partner's loop

3. Pull over partner's hand

4. Your string will come loose

Keeping an idiot amused

On one side of sheet of paper, write, "How do you keep an idiot amused for hours?," adding "P.T.O." (Please Turn Over) at the bottom of the paper.

Write exactly the same thing on the other side, then wait for someone to pick it up. Chances are that they will turn it over, then over again then, with luck, a couple more times before they realize that they are the idiot being kept amused!

The severed finger

Under one end of a large-sized matchbox or a cardboard jewelry box, make a finger-sized hole. Then dust your index finger with talcum powder to give it a white, lifeless look, and poke it through the hole where it should nestle on a bed of cotton wool. If you want to go the whole hog, red food coloring can be added to the "torn" base of the finger.

Close the box as well as you can (you can always cut a notch out of the outer shell) and then, with a suitably gory tale about how you found the severed digit, show your victim the finger. Having the finger on its side keeps your hand in a reasonably natural position, particularly if you disguise your digitally impaired state with your other hand.

As your victim stares, have the finger quiver and then rise to life.

To make blood more convincing, you should experiment with adding a brown tinge through the addition of a little green coloring.

If you're after truly realistic blood for plays or Halloween, mix up corn flour and water, then add some golden syrup. Add the red and green coloring to the mixture and, if it isn't going anywhere near young mouths, a little washing-up liquid too. Take care with food coloring, though. It can stain clothing, and your reputation as a responsible Dad.

Is it a bird?

This is a great practical joke to play with your kids rather than on them. When out in an area with lots of people, all stare upward at something that seems to fascinate you, occasionally pointing. Almost invariably, others will try to see what you're all looking at. They may even stop to get a better look.

If you manage to attract a few people, that's your cue to vamoose, leaving a group behind, none of whom wants to admit that they can't see what the others are so obviously looking at.

The mysterious pendulum

Kids usually like spooky stuff. So why not introduce them to a magic pendulum? It doesn't need to be anything more sophisticated than a weight on the end of six inches or so of string, or a necklace with a charm on it. Something pointy and not too heavy is best.

If you want to go the whole mystical hog, you can use ancient golden thread (picture wire) and a supernatural crystal (bits of an old chandelier you never got round to throwing away would be ideal). Turn down the lights and strew a few candles around to enhance the mood.

With their elbow resting on the table, the subject should hold the pendulum in one hand with the bob dangling just above the surface.

Get them to keep their hand still and concentrate hard on the bob. They should see if they can control it using only the hidden powers of their mind. If it begins moving, suggest they try to make it swing back and forward. Then sideways. How about in a circle? Now the other way. Now make it stop on command.

The weird thing is that, however hard you try not to move your hand, it does somehow make the pendulum do what your brain wants it to.

Once the pendulum can be controlled, things can get stranger still. Draw a circle

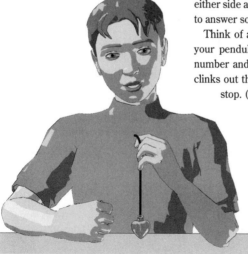

with "yes" at the top and bottom and "no" at either side and ask the power of the pendulum to answer some questions.

Think of a number up to 10, then suspend your pendulum in a glass. Think about the number and the pendulum will swing until it clinks out the number and then mysteriously stop. (Well, it did when we tried it!)

You can make up various games to invoke the power of the pendulum, such as hiding an object under one of several cups and seeing if the pendulum can find it. Sadly, it's not much use when you've lost the car keys or the TV remote.

10 Fun and games

AT SOME POINT, even the most indoor-loving Dad is going to have to step outside. It may involve taking the kids to the park, or the beach, or just mucking about in the garden: but there comes a time when the telly has to go off, and the Great Outdoors has to be faced in all its glory.

If you're one of those Dads for whom an exciting game of football involves a beer, a TV and an armchair, don't panic. Many of the games in this chapter entail little or no physical exercise on your part, although with luck, the little darlings will tire themselves out. As well as some that might be unfamiliar, we've also got some old favorites, injecting a spark of new life into them with some novel twists.

We've also included a set of indoor games that will turn a wet afternoon on its head. The emphasis here is on group and team activities, so there's plenty to choose from to keep your child's next birthday party bubbling along happily.

Tag

This must be one of the oldest and simplest of kids' games. The person who is "It" chases the others. If they catch anyone, they yell out "You're It" and that person then becomes "It."

There are, however, plenty of variations on the theme, each with different names depending on where they were learned. In *Freeze Tag*, whoever is touched does not become "It," but freezes in place and can be unfrozen again if one of the free players touches them. Along similar lines, a player who is tagged must stand with their legs apart and can only be freed if a player crawls through their legs. In some quarters, this is known as *Dirty Diaper Tag* or *Stuck in the Mud.*

Your turn to crawl through next!

Hospital Tag requires a tagged player to hold the spot where they were touched with one hand. They are now "It," but must keep their hand there while they try to tag other players. *Copycat Tag* requires every player to adopt the same posture, no matter how ridiculous, as "It." On sunny days, you can even play *Shadow Tag,* where "It" has to step on the shadows of the players in order to hand over the baton.

One variant, fondly remembered from our playground days, has players claiming sanctuary if they can get off the ground by standing or climbing on something. There is usually a set time limit, however, after which they can be tagged. Or the person who is "It" might shout out a substance which will make players safe, such as "Metal" or "Plastic." Anyone touching something of that material, though only one player per item, is safe.

In *Snake Tag*, for which you need a minimum of six players, each player holds the player in front around the waist. The head must try to tag the tail, a game that is as much fun to watch as it is to play.

Tennis cricket

The real game of cricket requires 22 people dressed in white, can take 5 days and has rules that would baffle a nuclear physicist. Tennis cricket, on the other hand, ideally suited to a park or the beach, is easy to pick up, requires no special clothes and can continue even if some people get bored and wander off or new ones turn up desperate to play.

Having gathered four players or more, all you need is a tennis ball and a racquet, preferably a small one, though you could use a piece of driftwood in a pinch. The batsman, circled by the other players, holds the racquet vertically, turning on the spot to face whichever fielder has the ball. That player should bowl underarm in an attempt either to hit the batsman's legs below the knee (in which case they're out) or to get them to hit the ball up for a catch.

Get the batsman out and you take over. As long as the ball is bowled underarm, it's perfectly acceptable to fake throws, hoping the batsman will leave their legs undefended for the real throw. Some people insist that the batsman cannot move their feet at all, making deliveries from the rear somewhat tricky to defend.

If you're playing on sand, a circle can be drawn out to mark a boundary. Get the ball over this and you score six if it doesn't touch the ground; four if it does. There are various ways to score runs. You can mark a spot that must be run to or, alternatively, the batsman must pass the racquet around their body as many times as he can before a fielder grabs the ball. One version allows fielders to pass the ball to anyone to bowl but, if this is combined with a ban on the batsman turning, the chances are somebody could end up in traction.

Blow football

It's all too easy to forget just how great some simple games can be. You've got straws, you've got a Ping-Pong ball, you've got a table. You've got yourself a blow football stadium. Set up something at each end of the table for the goals, boxes on their side or books masquerading as goalposts, and start blowing.

Kubb: the best outdoor game of all

Since we discovered the Swedish game of *Kubb*, we haven't been able to stop playing it. Luckily, everyone we've forced to try it likes it as much as we do, making it a mystery why it isn't more popular than football by now. It's the perfect game for a lawn or beach.

Unless you fancy popping round to our place for a game, you'll need a Kubb set. The chances are you won't have one lying at the back of your hall cupboard among all those unused tennis racquets, but it's pretty simple to make a set out of bits of wood: you need ten Kubbs, six throwing batons and one King. But if you flunked woodwork at school, a quick Web search should reveal one you can order.

A Viking game that the Swedes claim was once played with the bones of those they defeated, the playing area should be about 5 paces wide by 8 long, though it's easier for children if it's slightly smaller. With the King set up in the center, each team (up to six people) stands behind their baseline, along which are evenly spread five Kubbs.

One player from each team throws a baton toward the King. The nearest to the King without touching starts, remembering that anyone knocking the King over too early immediately loses that game.

Batons must be thrown underarm!

Each Kubb measures 7 × 7 × 15 cm

The throwing batons are 2·5 to 4 cm in diameter, and 30 cm long

The King measures 10 × 10 × 30 cm

Players can stand level with their furthest forward Kubb

The aim of the game is to knock down all the Kubbs in the rival half of the pitch and then topple the King.

Team A starts by throwing their batons underarm, end over end (no sideways, helicopter throws allowed), attempting to knock down as many of Team B's Kubbs as possible.

Before Team B can retaliate, they must throw any fallen Kubbs into Team A's half of the pitch between the King and the baseline.[1] Team A then stand up those Kubbs—now called Field Kubbs—where they landed.

Team B must knock down these Field Kubbs before they can go for the baseline Kubbs. It's fine if a baton knocks down more than one Kubb. But any baseline Kubbs accidentally knocked over before the Field Kubbs are toppled should be set upright again, unless the last Field Kubb has gone down with that very throw.

Team A must now throw any fallen Kubbs back to their opponents' half. If there are any Field Kubbs still standing on their side of the pitch, however, they can stand level with the furthest one when throwing their batons.[2]

Turns continue until one team has knocked down all their opponents' Kubbs. The players must then retreat to the baseline and use the rest of their turn to try to knock down the King and win the game. (The King can be toppled in the very first round only if two batons are left, a pretty unlikely event.)

The joy of Kubb is that players' fortunes wax and wane. One moment you're sure you're about to lose, the next you're on top again. Sometimes games are over in a few minutes, other times they last 20 minutes or longer.[3] It's one of those games that doesn't really make sense until you play it—and then it's hard to stop.

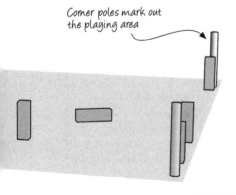

Corner poles mark out the playing area

1. They get two chances to throw the Kubbs back; if they miss both times, the other team places those Kubbs anywhere in their half a minimum of one baton's length from the King or a corner marker.

2. Kubbs themselves, however, must always be thrown from the baseline.

3. A good variation is to allow thrown Kubbs that hit each other to be built into towers—it makes them much easier to knock over, and can speed up sluggish games.

The Centipede

This variant of the *Wheelbarrow Race* is even sillier and more droll. It's best played on soft ground or even indoors if there's enough space. You need a couple of teams, each with a minimum of four players. Try to ensure that they are evenly matched, splitting kids of similar ages and adults.

Both teams should line up in a row and then get onto their hands and knees. With the exception of each leader, the players should put their hands on or around the waist or hips of the person in front. At the command, they head toward the finish line as quickly as they can. If the centipede breaks, the team must stop and reconnect before proceeding.

To make it harder, you can use a marker such as a tree or pile of clothes and make the two teams go around this before returning to the starting line.

Pass the water, please

If you've a good many kids to entertain outside on a hot day, why not re-create something of the atmosphere of *It's a Double Dare* with a game that's messy, frantic, and enormous fun. (Who says we watched too much TV when we were kids?) You'll need a paddling pool (any large water container will do), two identical buckets, two identical sponges, and a bunch of children prepared to get very wet.

To think I left the Great Barrier Reef for this . . .

Arrange them into two lines leading away from the paddling pool, with an empty bucket at the head of the line. On the word "Go," the person nearest the pool in each line saturates the sponge and then passes it along the line until the last person squeezes what's left of the water out into the bucket.

The sponge is then passed back to the paddling pool end—no throwing!—to be refilled. The winning team is the one that fills its bucket first.

Double Blind

A great, raucous game that can be played in the park, on the beach, or in any wide open space where the neighbors aren't going to complain about the noise.

Split up into two teams: each team chooses one person to be blindfolded (a sweater over the head works well if you haven't got any scarves at hand). Both blindfolded team members have to be guided, by shouts from their fellow team members, around an obstacle (a tree, for example) and back to the rest of the team.

Here's the fun part: both blindfolded competitors are trying to complete the course *at the same time*, with everyone on both teams yelling instructions simultaneously.

Not, perhaps, a game to be played near rose-bushes or on busy streets.

What's the time, Mr. Wolf?

This is an alternative to *Musical Statues*, a game that tends to degenerate into "You moved," "No I didn't," "You're out," "I'm not playing" arguments. Appoint a Wolf, a role for which Dads are eminently suited as it gives such scope for their untapped ability to overact shamelessly.

The Wolf stands with his back to the other players, who should begin at least 20 feet away. They call out, "What's the time, Mr. Wolf?" and the Wolf turns and shouts out a time, which must be something o'clock. The players advance a corresponding number of steps toward the Wolf. If he says "Two o'clock," for instance, they move two steps toward him.

As they get nearer to the Wolf and the tension rises, the players all know that the next time they ask, "What's the time, Mr. Wolf?," they might get the answer "DINNER TIME!" from a slavering Wolf who now chases them, trying to catch one before they reach the safety of the starting line. Depending on local rules, the person caught may become the Wolf or not.

Charades

This is one of the all-time great games for a decent-sized group. Kids love it. But we often find games are spoiled because of vagueness over the rules.

There should be two teams with adults and kids evenly split. One person must act, silently, a charade chosen by the other team. It can be a book (mime opening a book), a song (mime singing), a play (curtains drawing apart), a TV show (draw a box in the air), or a film (an old-fashioned hand-cranked movie camera).

Book   Song   TV show

Film   Play

If only adults are playing, suggestions might be as fiendish as *The Shorter Oxford English Dictionary,* but if you want to keep kids happy and absorbed, it's better to choose stuff they know well, such as favorite books or movies.

The mimer should indicate with their fingers the number of words in the title,

3 words   2 syllables   Little word

including "a" and "the." They can act out the whole thing (use a grand sweeping gesture to indicate you're going to do this), any of the words or part of any word. Words don't have to be acted out in order, but the mimer should indicate which word it is by holding up their fingers again.

To show how many syllables a word has (ensure before starting that everyone understands what a syllable is), put that number of fingers on the forearm. To act out a particular syllable, show that number of fingers of the forearm again. Four fingers in the air, three on the forearm followed by two on the arm indicates that they are to act out the second syllable of the fourth word, which has three syllables. If there's a little word (such as "a," "the," or "of"), show which it is with fingers, then draw the index finger and thumb together.

When someone guesses the right word, the mimer should point and nod at whoever got it right, giving a rapid wave of the hand if the person is close, but not quite there.

If you can't think how to act out a word you can try something that sounds like it—putting your hand to your ear indicates "sounds like." If the word needs to be shorter or longer, move your hands as if you're showing the size of a fish.

When playing with two, alternating, teams, everyone takes their turn in order. This does mean, however, that half the players are just sitting there at any one time. Our preferred method is for one player to start the ball rolling, performing a title given to him by someone else (probably Dad); thereafter, when a player guesses the correct title, it's *their* turn to act out a title, which is written down for them by the player who's just performed. If someone isn't getting enough turns, Dad can opt to slot them in as appropriate.

The Flippin' Fish

The kids should cut out paper, newspaper or tissue paper in the shape of a fat fish. All contestants must place their fish on the floor and stand behind it. On the word "Go!," they must flap a sheet of card or a magazine madly to make their fish head toward the finishing line or, alternatively, a plate onto which the fish must land. A great party game.

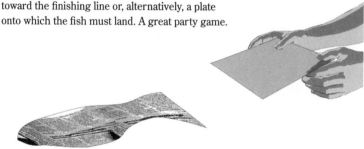

Who's in the Hat?

The problem with many games that involve trivia-style questions is that most children are at a massive disadvantage to the adults, having had far fewer years in which to accumulate the sort of nutty knowledge that is mainly useful only for playing trivia quizzes.

Most kids, however, *are* familiar with a prodigious number of celebrities and pop stars, making *Who's in the Hat?* a splendid family game. You'll need a one-minute timer (plundered from another board game if necessary).

Divide the players into a couple of equally able—or unable—teams. Each player writes five names of well-known people, who can be fictional, on slips of paper and drops them into the hat. One player from each team must then, without mentioning the name of the people in any way, try to get their teammates to guess who they're talking about. Each name guessed in the time wins the team a point.

Take it in turns until all the names are used up. A great spin on the game as it's traditionally played is to put the names back in and do it over: this time, however, players are restricted to saying just three words. Since these three words will probably be drawn from the previous, lengthy explanation, it's a test of memory and conciseness to see who can remember to whom those three words apply. And when that round is over, do it once more, but this time only one word can be uttered for each name.

Ibble Dibble

To our surprise, this utterly ridiculous student drinking game works brilliantly even without the injection of copious quantities of alcohol. You do, however, need to remember to save a cork or two from your last bottle of wine. Before the game commences, this needs to be burned on the outside by being held in a flame. Be sure not to burn plastic corks!

Form your players into a circle and assign each player a number in order. The first player must say, word perfect, "*Ibble Dibble Number One with no Dibble Ibbles, calling Ibble Dibble Number . . .*" At this point they choose another player, calling them by their number, and continuing, ". . . *with no Dibble Ibbles.*" That player, say Number Three, must continue, "*Ibble Dibble Number Three with no Dibble Ibbles, calling Ibble Dibble Number . . .*" and choose another player, and so on.

Any mistakes and the error-prone player must have their face marked with the cork. Each player must add the number of the marks on their own face as well as the number of marks on the player

After the kids have gone to bed, the game can be played in its original form

they are calling. Every error means another black mark. So player two with three marks must say to player five with one mark, "*Ibble Dibble Number Two with three Dibble Ibbles, calling Ibble Dibble number Five with one Dibble Ibble,*" and so on. As things go on, it becomes ever harder to remember how many marks you have on your own face and, while the marks might begin by being spots on the cheeks, they may later be on the nose, or black eyes, or mustaches.

And once the kids have gone to bed, the adults—no doubt needing another burned cork—can open a bottle and play the game as it's meant to be played, with drinks as forfeits for mistakes.

Island Hopping

Take the cushions off your sofa. Place them strategically around the room—or interspersed through several rooms, if you have enough cushions—and challenge your kids to get from one end of the island chain to the other, without stepping on the floor. It's a great indoor physical game, as long as you remember to remove any priceless Ming vases and family heirlooms first.

Outdoors, the same game can be played using towels or clothing. If your partner objects (*if???*), you can try using newspapers, as long as it's not too windy. If you have any trees handy, these can be used for swinging on to overcome larger gaps.

To extend the game further and make it more of a challenge for a wider age range, start with a large number of islands and then remove them, one at a time, after each successful completion of the chain by all the children playing. Even younger kids will enjoy watching their elders making their way across a course that defeated them.

The Jell-O game

With everyone in a circle, a die should be thrown in turn. If anyone gets a six, they must don a waiting hat, scarf and gloves and try to eat their way through a bowl of Jell-O with a knife and fork. If you want to make it truly fiendish, then mittens or oven gloves can be used.

Only one minute is allowed before the die is thrown again. The game ends when the Jell-O does. Often played with a bar of chocolate instead of the Jell-O, it's a simple party game that kids find hilarious. You can also put the gloves to use in *Pass the Parcel* to make it that much trickier.

11 Kindergarten kids

IF YOUR KIDS ARE STILL IN DIAPERS and endlessly fascinated by a revolving mobile tinkling "Twinkle Twinkle Little Star," the chances are that even your best-rehearsed magic tricks will go unappreciated. But at some stage, babies change into children and you can wheel out some of that Dad stuff you've been desperately waiting to try.

Younger children are a less demanding audience than their older siblings. You don't need to be an expert at sleight of hand to pretend you've plucked off their nose by sticking your thumb between your first and second fingers. The downside, however, is that they will want to experience their favorites again . . . and again . . . and again.

The younger kids are, the more physical they'll want their games to be. But that's OK: you're still young yourself and in your prime. They won't have crushed the life out of you for a good few years yet.

This Is the Way the Ladies Ride

There are countless nursey rhymes and songs with accompanying actions to delight younger children. "Itsy bitsy spider," for instance, seems to be hard-wired into all adults' brains.

"Itsy bitsy spider climbed up the water spout (walk your hand up their arm), down came the rain (waggle your fingers as you lower them to simulate rain) and washed the spider out (throw your arms out), Out came the sun and dried up all the rain (make a circle with your hands for the sun) so the itsy bitsy spider climbed up the spout again (again walk your hand up their arm)."

Of the action songs, our favorite is the knee-bouncing rhyme "This Is the Way the Ladies Ride." It has the great merit that you don't really need to sing but can instead do a Rex Harrison "can't sing, won't sing" impersonation.

Let the rider hang onto your hands as you raise your legs onto your toes in time with the words, four times to each line, so that each lift of the legs coincides with the stress of the words.

A gentle bounce should accompany this verse:

This is the way the ladies ride
Trippety-tee, trippety-tee
This is the way the ladies ride
Trippety-trippety-tee.

Lift your knees higher:

This is the way the gentlemen ride
Gallopy-gallop, gallopy-gallop
This is the way the gentlemen ride
Gallopy-gallopy-gallop.

For the last verse, make the riding "terrain" really rough:

This is the way the farmers ride
Hobbledee-hoy, hobbledee-hoy
This is the way the farmers ride
Hobbledee-hoy and down in the DITCH.

On "DITCH" move your knees apart so the child falls a little way. Repeated a few times, it's amazing how tiring this can be. For you, that is, rather than for the child —who'll still be begging for more after twenty minutes.

The Tickle Robot

On your palm, draw the numbers 1 to 4 and the letter R. Stand stock still, with a vacant expression on your face, gazing into the middle distance (fathers of young babies will find this comes quite naturally). Robot though you may now be, you are a robot in standby mode.

Encourage a child to experiment with pressing the numbers to see what happens. As a number is pressed, come to life, standing tall but with your control pad (hand) still in reach. Another press and you should advance toward your "controller," your aim being to pick up, tickle or do whatever you think the child will like. Change your actions as they press the buttons unless they press the "R" for "reset" button, in which case you should return to standby mode. Move in jerky, robotic spurts, and try to keep your face entirely passive—this really helps the robotic effect.

Young kids seem to love the playful scariness of the tickle robot. You know you've got it right if, moments after claiming they can't face being tickled any more, they press another button. Once they've got the hang of it, you don't even need to write on your palm; just holding out your hand should alert them to the game. You can add endless variations and wind yourself up with an imaginary key if this helps move the action along.

Find me a yellow flower . . .

. . . a red leaf, a stone the size of your thumbnail, and a twig the length of your little finger. Ready . . . Go! And off they scamper to do your bidding, leaving you to enjoy that postprandial cup of coffee while you chat with your friends. It's an activity that requires absolutely no effort on your part, and will keep the little darlings happily occupied for ages.

The garden on a plate

A good activity on a sunny day. The aim is to plunder the garden for bits of grass, earth, interesting leaves, small flowers and twigs, and to build a garden using a plastic plate as a base. It encourages creativity and small children take a real pride in their creations.

Simon Says

We all remember this one from our childhoods, yet it's just as much fun for kids as it ever was. They have to do everything you tell them—putting their hands on their shoulders, sticking out their tongues, standing on one leg—as long as the command begins "Simon says." If it doesn't, then they must *not* obey the request, which makes it particularly enjoyable if it's "go and get a chocolate biscuit from the cupboard."

In Simon's household, the children always do everything he says as a matter of course. Or so Simon says.

Smashing fun

You've spent an hour and a half building a spaceship out of Lego bricks. The creation is finished, and it's a stunning work of engineering. The problem is: what do you do with it now? You can't really keep it, partly because there's nowhere to put it and partly because you're going to need the bricks again for the next creation. But mainly, of course, because it really isn't *that* good a model, and you know you could make a much better one next time around.

The best solution is to treat it the way you'd treat any spaceship, and throw it through the air. Sure, it will smash on impact—but that's exactly the point. Kids get told off every time they break household objects, so it's a great treat for them to be told they're allowed to destroy something for once, especially something as destructively extravagant as a thousand-piece Lego model.

The leaning tower of Lego

Now that you've got a floor full of Lego bricks, what better use can you put them to than to make a tower as big as your child? If they're young enough to have Duplo, use these as the base: for, amazingly, not only can you build Duplo on top of Lego, you can also build Lego on top of Duplo. These toy designers really thought that one out.

Kids are amazed when they manage to create something bigger than they are—it's a kind of benchmark of what's within their reach. It's a fairly mindless activity, so you can easily do it at four o'clock in the morning (or whatever time your sleepless toddler has woken you up).

When the model's finished—topple it over and smash it, of course. Then they can have a go at building it again themselves, while you "rest your eyes" for a few minutes on the couch.

The handkerchief rabbit

Open out a handkerchief and run it through your closed hand, making it long and thin. Tie a knot a third of the way along and fluff out the smaller section. This will be the rabbit's ears (even though there's only one of them).

With the ears pointing up your arm toward your elbow, cradle the rabbit in the palm of your outstretched hand and stroke it with your other hand to conceal what you're doing. With the middle finger of your rabbit-holding hand, flick the knot to make the rabbit jump along your arm.

As the rabbit jumps, affect surprise and, delaying just a fraction of a second, pull the naughty rabbit back down by its tail. Stroke it again for a while to calm it, only to find it jumping away again when you least expect it. Although this is something younger children love, it is surprising how fascinated by the rabbit even supposedly cool teenagers can be.

If you don't carry a handkerchief, it will work with cuddly toys that are big enough to hide your fingers but small enough to travel up your forearm.

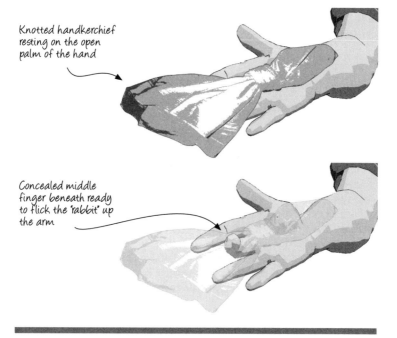

Knotted handkerchief
resting on the open
palm of the hand

Concealed middle
finger beneath ready
to flick the 'rabbit' up
the arm

Teensy Rider

Sit the child on your knees, facing away. Hold up your arms, fists clenched, for them to grab hold of your fists.

They're now holding the handlebars of a powerful motorbike, the noise supplied by you. Faster and faster you go, leaning into ever steeper corners, going up steep hills only to plunge down the other side, hitting potholes, bumping along dirt tracks, even attempting the odd jump. You can also be a rollercoaster, with your folded arms as the safety bar.

Not surprisingly for beginners, almost all rides end in a crash. If, when they hit their teens, they start wearing bike leathers, don't blame us.

Hunt the Fluff

It really did used to be *Hunt the Fluff*, in the days when young Simon had a fluffy bedspread and Mrs. Smith came to babysit. There aren't many fluffy bedspreads around now, so you might prefer to call the game Hotter or Colder. It doesn't have to be fluff anyway. Anything tiny will do. At bedtime, get the child to hide whatever they want you to look for in their room. It's a great way of making recalcitrant children keen to clamber into bed.

Only once they've snuggled down should you hunt for it. As you prowl around their bedroom peering into nooks and crannies, they need to tell you when you're getting "hotter" or "colder" or, ultimately, "boiling" or "freezing." You can spin it out by deliberately going the wrong way and misunderstanding them.

The other way of playing the game, of course, is to make the child do the hunting while you give directions. Steve uses this method for prolonging the anticipation before Freddy and Joe open their birthday presents, by first concealing them around the bedroom. It's become so popular that they'll even ask for their presents to be hidden in this way—and it's certainly one way of slowing down the annual frenzied attack on the wrapping paper.

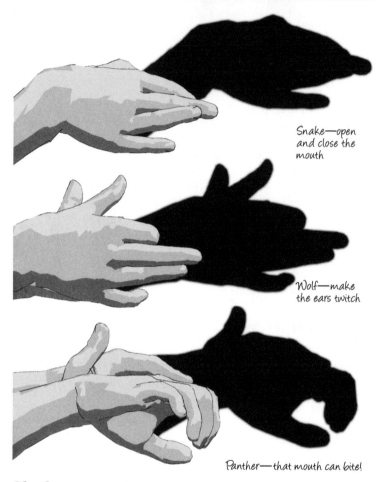

Snake—open and close the mouth

Wolf—make the ears twitch

Panther—that mouth can bite!

Shadow puppets

Fun and easy to do, with a little practice. For very young children, try sitting on the floor cross-legged with them sitting in your lap directly beneath a ceiling light (halogen spotlights are best), and perform the shadows on the floor in front of them. It's much more immediate than projecting onto a wall.

Some of these require two hands, and they're harder to do (and won't work

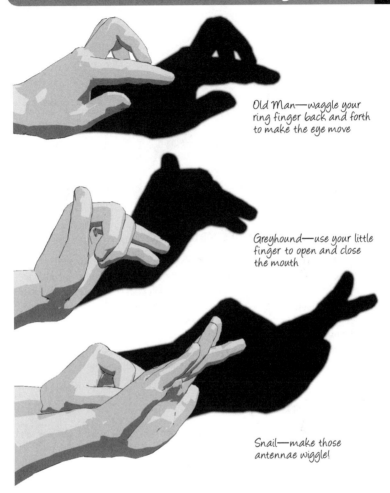

Old Man—waggle your ring finger back and forth to make the eye move

Greyhound—use your little finger to open and close the mouth

Snail—make those antennae wiggle!

when your child is in your lap). But with the single-handed shadows you can do a different one with each hand, and make them fight each other. Also try simple shadowplays, such as making a basic shadow of your outstretched hand—the fingers can pop open one by one—and having one of the animals "eat" the fingers one at a time. Younger children find this hilarious.

Wiping the smile off your face

Move your flat, open hand from the top of your head to your chin quickly, changing a smile to a frown as you do so. Bring the hand back up and smile again. It's a particularly good ruse for cheering up small children who find themselves affronted or just in a bad mood, and will even work reasonably well with older kids as well. Getting kids to smile is the first step in helping them to get themselves out of a bad mood.

Just remember where you are. It may work wonders with little ones, but it's likely to cause bewilderment if you're with your mates in the pub.

Dad, the action toy

Press your nose and have your tongue pop out. Pull your right ear and, simultaneously, bend your tongue to the right, as if it's the ear tug that is doing it. Pull your left ear and have it go the other way. Press your nose again—and the tongue disappears.

A nice variation is to press your nose, tweak your ear or operate another control point, while making an entirely unrelated part of your body respond to the action. A leg could pop up, a foot start tapping, an elbow twitch, and so on. You should try to express complete surprise at these effects, as if they're entirely involuntary.

After a while, your child will probably want to operate the "buttons" themselves. Let them—unless they're in their teens and angry that you won't let them have their ears pierced.

12 It's a Dad's world

WE'RE THE FIRST TO ADMIT that there are some things Dads just aren't biologically cut out for. If it was left to us, our children would still be wearing clothes they grew out of three years ago and begging us never to dish up beans on toast again.

But there are some areas in which Dads excel. With our trusty Swiss Army penknives always at the ready, you can be sure that Dad will fix that broken gadget—or, at the very least, to tell you that it's so far beyond repair that you *have* to get a new one immediately, especially since there's a new souped-up turbo version available at a special introductory price.

Dads are also expected to be able to teach their kids to do things. The trouble is, we have to learn them first, so a bit of secret practice is needed when everyone's gone to bed. That way, when your child says "Dad, can you juggle?," they'll be truly impressed when you toss the contents of the fruit bowl in the air and catch them all on the way down.

How to teach a child to ride a bike

"Of course I won't let go," fibs even the most doting Dad, puffing away madly as he runs behind his child's bike. A moment later, he takes his hand away, praying that the child will stay upright. Some do. Some don't. The loss of trust between those who fall and their fathers is psychiatry's future gain.

There is a better way. Children are instinctively able to "scoot," so get them used to the bike by scooting first. Once they grow out of riding with training wheels to keep them upright, remove the bike's pedals with either a spanner or allen wrench, depending on the bike. Then lower the seat until your child can sit

Lower seat using the nut underneath the saddle

Take the pedals off at the front gear wheel

with both feet comfortably flat on the ground.

Now they can scoot along using both feet, lifting them from the ground between pushes. This way, they learn how to balance and turn on two wheels without simultaneously having to cope with the destabilizing circular motion of the pedals. Once they are happily scooting and turning, you can replace the pedals, knowing that the child is already adept with every other aspect of the bike.

Remember where you put the pedals when you take them off!

Child's feet should be able to touch the ground

How to remember your kids' birthdays

One thing you must never, ever, *ever* forget is your child's birthday. It's perfectly possible that they will help you out, reminding you of the forthcoming date at frequent intervals and offering helpful hints as to suitable presents. But this can't be relied upon, so Dads are forced to use such unreliable things as memory, diaries, electronic organizers and the like.

Now that credit cards have four-digit PIN numbers that can be altered to any combination, why not amend your number to that of your child's birthday? That way, you're very unlikely to forget.

More than one child? Simple. Get another credit card for each successive addition to the family. You'll need them.

How to bark like a dog

It is surprisingly easy to learn to bark. With a little practice, you'll be able to summon up a dog that will fool not only kids, but quite a few canines as well.

Get a deep "rrrr" vibrating at the back of the throat. As you're doing this, you should say the word "rough" loudly, emphasizing the latter, "uff" part of the sound. The "rough" should come out

Spot the difference

very quickly, like a mini-explosion. Make sure you open your mouth wide as you do it.

Experiment with pitch until you find the level that best suits you. We're both yappy mongrels rather than Westminster Kennel Club contenders, but you may find your inner dogginess as something more substantial.

It might be best to practice somewhere quiet—like a padded cell. Even as expert barkers, the first one each time can be under par. So we prefer to bark offstage, enticing curious kids to come running. When they arrive, they find us already looking for the dog they heard but which, mysteriously, can't be found.

How to untangle puppet strings

In a perfect world, children would tidy their puppets away with the strings neatly gathered together and elegantly looped over the control bar.

Sadly, the world of children is rarely so well ordered. So it's up to Dad to sort out a tangled mess of strings . . . again. What's most frustrating is that you know it must be possible to reverse whatever's been done, but it isn't long before your brain is reeling in a way it hasn't since you last played with a Rubik's Cube.

The tangle often results from nothing more than the control bar being flipped over when the puppet was put away and then flipped once more when it was picked up again. The first thing to do is see if turning the bar over will sort it out.

If it doesn't, then unsnag the strings from the puppet and the bar so you have only one loose knot of strings in between to sort out. Instead of pulling at them aimlessly, choose one of the strings—say the rear one—and try to get that free. If you can, use it as a pivot, twisting the bar one way and the other to untwist the other strings.

If this doesn't work, then remember the Dad's maxim: if at first you don't succeed—cheat. Untie one or more strings from the control bar, sort them out and then refasten them. If you need new string, fishing line works well. And in future, only buy modern puppets with readily detachable, color-coded strings.

As a last resort, untie a string to untangle it.

How to untie stubborn knots

Shoelaces, bathing suit strings, and the like have a nasty tendency to get badly knotted up, particularly when the knots have been tied by small fingers in a hurry. To a child, the untying process involves pulling any stray ends they can find—which only makes the problem worse.

The solution is to rub the knot firmly between your thumb and forefinger, using a slight rotary motion with your thumb. This action can generally persuade even the most awkward knot to yield to your touch.

How to tie shoelaces so they don't come undone

Walk down the road with a gang of children and you can pretty well guarantee that at any given moment at least one is kneeling down doing a shoelace up. It slows down family outings more than anything else, yet it's wholly avoidable.

Begin tying the shoelace as normal with the over and under starting knot. The next stage is usually to make a loop from one of the laces, then wind the other lace around it before poking it through the opening to make a second loop.

Instead, get them to wind the second lace around the first loop not once but twice before poking it through the opening. This shoelace won't come undone until you want it to.

How to keep a cardboard box closed

You want the box shut but you've no tape on hand, or you're deluded enough to think you're only putting it away for a short while. Easy when you know how.

Choose to go clockwise or counterclockwise. Take one flap and overlap the next flap slightly. Keeping that corner in position, ensure that the second flap goes outside the next flap around, again overlapping it slightly. Do the same for the other two corners.

Once you've ensured that each flap overlaps the successive corner, begin working all the inside flaps downward.

The cardboard will tend to bend a little, but suddenly you'll find all the flaps dropping into place at the same time and, *voilà*—a perfectly sealed cardboard box.

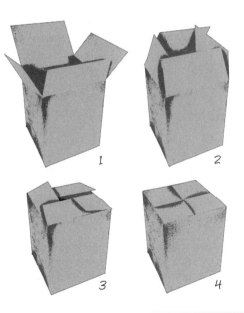

How to juggle

If you've always wanted to juggle, learning so you can entertain your children is the perfect excuse.

Proper juggling balls can be handy. They're like spherical bean bags and have a welcome tendency to stay where they land, so you don't spend half your time hunting around under the sofa. You can learn comfortably with bean bags, or any softish balls two to three inches across. It's best not to use fruit just yet unless you fancy explaining why everything in the bowl is so badly bruised.

Get used to holding three balls right from the start. Hold one in the palm of your right hand. Make a curved V-sign with your left hand, and put one ball in it and another in the palm, held there by your thumb and third and fourth fingers.

The first stage is to practice throwing the ball in your left V up and to the right so it describes an arc, peaking around your eyeline, and dropping into a corresponding V in the right hand. Then throw it back the same way. The aim is to do this over and over again while looking ahead, not at your hands.

Get used to moving your hands from the outset. Your left hand should move counterclockwise from your point of view, largely from the wrist, the right hand clockwise. It isn't quite a circle, more the flatter sort of wave a lazy King would give the plebs from his carriage. This is how you avoid the balls hitting each other in the air.

In stage two, just as the first ball hits its peak, you should throw the ball from your right hand to your left hand. Initially, it doesn't matter if you're almost putting it in your left hand, just so long as you get used to getting rid of the ball and getting your hand back into position in time to catch the ball heading to your right hand. You should only progress beyond this stage, though, when both balls are reaching your eyeline every time.

The third stage is to add the third ball, throwing it as the second reaches its apex. Catch each one as it lands so you end up with two balls in the right hand and one in your left. When you have perfected this, try to keep going, throwing each ball as the one heading for that hand reaches its apex.

Don't be stingy with your throws. Although it's tempting not to throw the balls very high, in fact the higher they're thrown (within reason) the easier it becomes.

You'll be tempted to walk forward to chase your balls as they fly through the air: try juggling while facing a wall at first, to prevent this happening.

Learning to juggle takes time and practice —a lot of it—but once

you can do it, it's like riding a bike; you can do it for life. It might be best to become proficient with three balls before you move on to juggling swords, flaming torches or chainsaws.

The painless way to learn to ski

Making people learn to ski by balancing them precariously on two long planks of wood plonked down on slippery snow is akin to trying to get kids to ride a bike without going the training wheel route first. It's not only tricky, but could put somebody off for life.

Instead, ask your instructor—or the children's—to start off with snow blades. They're much shorter than conventional skis so everything is easier: keeping your balance; maneuvering; even getting up again when you fall over. With blades, confidence—and ability—comes more quickly. When you've got the hang of it, it's then fairly easy to transfer to proper skis. Kids already adept on roller blades should find ski blades easy to learn.

Using this method, Simon—hardly the sportiest of individuals—went from novice to tackling a couple of black runs in just four and a half days. Showing off? Sure, but everyone else is bored of hearing about it so it's your turn now.

Misconceptions

You don't always have to tell your children the truth. Sometimes a white lie is better than exposing them to the harsh realities of life. Sometimes, though, it's just plain fun to mess with their heads by telling them some outrageous whoppers.

Here are a few of our favorite misconceptions spread by mischievous parents. We'd like to think some people reached adulthood still believing that:

- Some breeds of cows have two legs shorter so that they can graze more easily on hillsides. On the flat, they simply go round in circles.

- Sheep are just woolly pigs.

- Just as hens lay eggs, so pigs lay sausages.

- Pigs can fly. But they're very lazy so they don't do it often.

- Sheep's wool shrinks when it rains and peels off so the farmer can collect it.

- Zebras are horses that have been painted with stripes so the farmer knows who they belong to.

- Electricity pylons are spaceships left behind after a Martian invasion was defeated.

- Birds don't get electrocuted when they land on pylons because they have rubber feet (or else hop quickly from leg to leg so they don't make a circuit).

- Bees make honey and wasps make jam.

- Rabbits can fly by flapping their ears very quickly.

- There's a parallel universe the other side of mirrors where people exactly like us do exactly the same things.

- It will be much easier to travel to China when they finish the tunnel through the middle of the Earth.

- Your toys come alive when you're asleep.

- By staying in the bath when the water's running out, you risk going down the drain with all the rest of the naughty children.

- A little man lives at the back of the fridge to turn the light on when we open the door.

Broken or battery?

When something stops working, how do you tell whether the battery has run down or if it's kaput? It's intensely irritating to buy yet more batteries for some power-greedy gizmo, only to discover it has given up the ghost for good (usually the first week after the warranty runs out).

Battery testers are useful, but aren't so handy for devices such as watches that need specialist help to replace their batteries. Instead, place the object somewhere with a source of gentle warmth, like in the laundry room or on a radiator. If a watch, warmed overnight, starts working again you know that all it needs is a battery replacement.

Ovens, conventional or microwave, are not suitable places to put batteries. In fact, doing so can be incredibly dangerous. So don't do it.

How to teach a child to skip rope

To teach a child to skip, get them to throw the rope over their head so it lands on the ground in front of them. Have them step forward over it. Then get them to do it again . . . and again . . . and again.

When they are adept at this, get them to jump forward over the rope each time. Speed the process up until suddenly they're skipping rope.

How to appear in family photographs

In every family, however technologically competent, there's usually only one person who takes responsibility for the camera. Whether it's a Dad or a Mum, they'll be the one who takes it along on holidays, to the beach, or gets it out on birthdays —which means they're guaranteed never to appear in family photographs.

All modern cameras have a self-timer, which gives you just enough time to run around the back and pose with your family. But unless you carry a tripod in your pocket, you'll find that setting up the camera is a nightmare.

A cushion, pillow or even a bunched-up sock makes a good "tripod," allowing you to support the camera and angle it toward the scene. Some enterprising camera shops are even selling overpriced bean bags precisely for this purpose.

Arrange your family in front of the lens, making sure they leave a space for you to slot into. Then—and here's the important bit—*angle the camera up* a

few degrees. You're likely to be the tallest person in the photograph, and if you compose the scene perfectly for the arrangement without you in it, you'll find all your pictures have the top of your head cropped off. Press the shutter, and then run like hell. And remember to smile: most of Steve's family snapshots show a perfectly composed grouping with a flustered, panicked Dad peering anxiously at the flashing timer light.

How to make a barbecue without poisoning your family

If there's one thing above all else that sorts out Dads from Mums, it's the barbecue. As soon as the weather turns nice, Dads who had trouble even finding the kitchen all through the winter suddenly start comparing marinade recipes and stocking up on wooden skewers.

Every Dad has his own distinctive barbecue ritual. We don't want to cramp your style. But there are a few pointers to make the experience less stressful.

First, light the barbecue a long time before everyone starts feeling hungry. Even the most carefully prepared fire will take 45 minutes to reach full strength, and if you wait until you've opened your second beer you'll find your kids have already escaped to McDonald's. (Avoid those all-in-one charcoal bags. They're done long before the food.)

Barbecued sausages always go down well, but if they're charcoal on the outside and salmonella pink on the inside you risk them coming up again in the middle of the night. Your safest bet is to *boil* sausages for ten minutes first: that way you know they'll be cooked all the way through, so you can just take them off when they change color. Boiling chicken portions doesn't work so well, but stick them in the microwave for ten minutes first and you'll ward off the worst of the unfriendly bacteria.

It's a sad fact, but barbecues always reach their peak just when you've finished cooking. But there's still time for your *pièce de résistance*: the barbecued banana. Here's the recipe: take a banana. Don't peel it—it's ready-wrapped. Place it on the barbecue. Take it off when it goes black, slice it open (it'll be too mushy to peel) and serve. And that's it. Implausible though it sounds, they're truly delicious.

The wonders of candle wax

You may have thought candles were only used for grown-up dinner parties, but the resourceful Dad will press all those one-inch stubs into service long after the guests have departed.

Rubbed on saw blades, the wax will ensure they cut smoothly through even the toughest wood. Rub a candle around a screw before driving it into a piece of wood or a Rawlplug, and it will screw home that much more easily. Best of all, though, is to rub candle wax on the metal runners of your kids' sleds—they'll glide over the snow even faster.

Knots: bowline

This is a great way of making a loop at the end of a rope. Tough and easy to make, good for swinging from a tree. This one's known as the King of Knots, and is recommended by the FAA for tying down light aircraft.

Make a small
loop in the rope

Pass the end
through the loop

Pass it under the
top end . . .

. . . then through the
loop and tighten

Knots: clove hitch (1)

A very good knot for attaching ropes to tree branches. This one's also useful for tying ropes onto a pole when you can't easily get to the end of the pole. Don't use this one where the pole can twist, or the knot will slip.

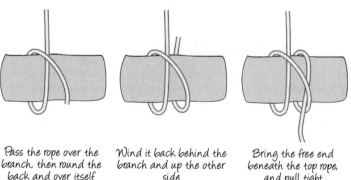

Pass the rope over the
branch, then round the
back and over itself

Wind it back behind the
branch and up the other
side

Bring the free end
beneath the top rope,
and pull tight

Knots: reef

The easiest way to join two ropes together. It's really just two opposing granny knots, but here's the correct way to make it so it won't easily come undone.

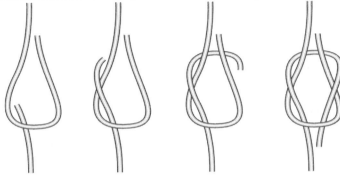

Make a loop with one rope, bring the other beneath it

Lift the second rope over the first . . .

. . . and around the back of it

Bring the free end through the loop and tighten

Knots: clove hitch (2)

Unlike the first clove hitch, this one's easier to tie when you *can* get to the free end of a pole or tree stump. Best for tying up boats, as it can be lifted off easily.

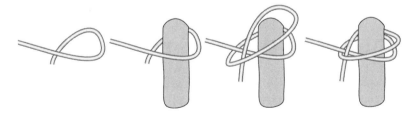

Make a simple loop, passing the free end of the rope beneath

Lift it over the pole or stump

Make exactly the same loop again with the free end beneath

Lift this one over the pole, and pull the whole thing tight

How to get children to go to sleep

The art of telling bedtime stories is one that's in danger of dying out, as live narrators are increasingly usurped by tapes, CDs and radio plays for children downloaded from the Internet and played back on iPods.

But storytelling is a great way of getting children—particularly younger ones—to relax and into a drowsy condition where they're ready for sleep. It doesn't have to be about enchanted forests, fairy princesses and magical beasts: the stories kids like best are those that describe their own lives.

Always begin with "Once upon a time." It's a time-honored tradition that will immediately put them in the right frame of mind for what's to come, and should get the eyelids drooping straightaway.

After that, we find the best method is to talk through the events of the day, step by step, beginning with breakfast (or teeth cleaning, face washing and sock-finding, if you think you're going to be in for a long session) and then continuing through each meal, outing and activity. It may sound dull, but that's the point: resist the temptation to embroider the facts.

Here's the clever part: when you get to the present time in your narrative, just *keep on going*. So deal with getting into pajamas, climbing into bed, then discuss Dad telling the story, and talk about how the child rolls onto their side, closes their eyes, and slips into a deep, deep sleep. With any luck, by that stage they'll simply follow the instructions and will be fast asleep.

Even if they don't drop straight off, the exercise will have helped them to sort out the day's activities into a logical and categorized order, encouraging relaxation and drowsiness. And the feeling of satisfaction you get when tiptoeing from the room is boundless.

The painless removal of splinters

In the majority of splinter episodes, there's no necessity for needles or tweezers. Providing just a little of the splinter is protruding, reduce tears and fears by simply sticking a piece of scotch tape over the splinter. Peel the tape off carefully and the splinter should come with it.

If this solution doesn't work, then try a fine pair of tweezers. Research the splinter-acquiring incident first: a little elementary deduction as to the angle of entry should ensure that all your efforts go toward pulling the thing out, rather than pushing it further in.

First aid: the psychological approach

When children hurt themselves, the one thing they want is a Mum. Any Mum will do, as long as she's huggable and carries one of those paramedic kits all Mums seem to keep in their handbags (aspirin, Band-Aid, bars of chocolate, and so on). But what's a Dad to do when there's no Mum to hand?

As long as the child isn't actually bleeding copiously or unconscious, the chances are the wound or bruise is more a question of hurt pride than injured bones. Humor, we find, really can be the best medicine.

That's not to say that you should laugh at their misfortunes: far from it. Take each incident perfectly seriously. Begin by looking at the bruised elbow, for

Stage 1   Stage 2   Stage 3

example, and scratching your chin. "Hmm," you say, donning your best bedside manner, "can you do this?" Bend your own elbow, or touch a finger to the affected part. Sniffling, the child will follow suit.

"OK," you continue, "how about this?" Perform something slightly silly—such as crossing your arms behind your back, or scratching your ear. This stage should just be within the bounds of medical possibility. Keep this up, performing sillier and sillier actions—sticking your fingers in your ears is a good one—all the while keeping a straight poker face. Before long, it's your child who will be laughing, and they'll forget they were ever injured.

Best to know where the local hospital is, though, just in case.

If it's broken—fix it

Few abilities define the competent Dad as much as the ability to mend things when they go wrong. What's needed is a heady mix of experience, confidence, and a willingness to take things apart on the grounds that if they're broken anyway, you can't make it any worse.

A small amount of knowledge can help immensely. Here are a few pointers to help you to mend a range of household objects.

Video recorders

Unplug from the outlet first. Then look at the back or side, and you should find one or two screws that hold the lid in place: unscrew these, and the whole lid should lift off. The machine may well be beyond repair, but if you find its innards to be full of Playmobil characters, dried toast, and final demands from the IRS, then you know someone's been using it as a mail slot again. Turn it upside down and shake it, but don't touch anything inside.

Heads will roll

The plastic heads of Action Man, Barbie, and Bratz dolls seem to fly off with the merest provocation, and all your pressing and grunting won't get them back on. The trick is to soften the neck aperture in really hot water for a few minutes first: this should make it pliable enough to slip the head back on.

Stopped watches

Good watches need a special tool to get them undone. But experienced Dads won't buy their kids decent watches, knowing that they'll be lost almost immediately anyway. Cheap watches look like they unscrew, but the backs can be often prised off with a knife: look for a tiny raised portion about a quarter inch long on the rim, which conceals a slight

Turning lugs are often fake

Look for a small indentation

gap below it. If you get the back off, most often you'll find the problem is simply that the battery has been shaken loose, and can easily be put back into position.

Toy soldiers

It all depends what they're made of. If the surface is hard and waxy, they're best glued with plastic model cement; if they're soft and shiny, they're probably polythene, which won't glue so well. A heated pin, pushed through the broken part into the body, can fix an arm, head or leg back in place.

Cassette tapes

It's infuriating when your child's favorite tape breaks. Here's how to mend it: pull both ends clear of the cassette, and turn them over so the underside is upward. Stick a piece of Scotch tape across the tape (the "invisible" variety works best) and then trim both sides of the Scotch tape with sharp scissors. Should be good for a few more car journeys!

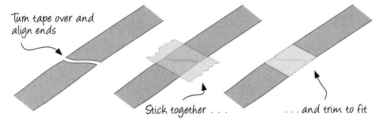

Turn tape over and align ends

Stick together . . .

. . . and trim to fit

DVDs

If your DVD is skipping, it may well be dirty rather than scratched. Wash it under warm water, and dry with a towel from the center outward—not around in a circle, as this is more likely to deepen any scratches there may be.

Chairs and small tables

You spend mealtimes begging kids not to tip back in their chair, and then the whole thing collapses. Except it's always *your* chair that breaks, not theirs. Use a quick-drying wood glue, but don't try to squeeze it into tiny gaps: pull the whole chair apart, and start again. If you don't have any clamps, tie the chair up with string and wind a stick through it to tighten the string until the wood glue has fully set (overnight is best). Then swap your chair for one of theirs.

Need more? Meet the authors and other Dads to suggest techniques,
exchange tips, or just chat about the whole Dad thing:

www.bethecoolestdad.com